# Harnessing Cosmic Energy

A Beginner's Guide to New Age Spiritual Practices"

Ellie Bloom

Copyright © 2023 by Ellie Bloom

All rights reserved.

No portion of this book may be reproduced in any form without written permission from the publisher or author, except as permitted by U.S. copyright law.

# Contents

1. Introduction — 1
2. Foundations of New Age Thought — 3
3. Understanding Cosmic Energy — 12
4. Meditation and Cosmic Energy — 25
5. Cosmic Energy Healing Practices — 43
6. Manifesting with Cosmic Energy — 58
7. Integrating Practices into Daily Life — 72
8. Advanced Concepts in Cosmic Energy — 89
9. Continuing Your Spiritual Journey — 98
10. Conclusion — 111

# 1

# Introduction

Welcome to the vibrant world of New Age spirituality, where an exciting concept takes center stage: cosmic energy. Imagine a universe interconnected by a vast, pulsating energy source that courses through all living things, linking us to the cosmos and each other. New Age spirituality sees this cosmic energy as a universal force influencing our physical, emotional, and spiritual well-being.

So, why does cosmic energy matter in the grand tapestry of our lives? In the realm of New Age philosophy, it's not just an abstract idea – it holds the potential to transform and enhance our daily experiences. Picture tapping into this cosmic energy as a way to align yourself with the natural rhythms of the universe, fostering balance, healing, and personal growth.

Consider meditation as a gateway, allowing you to quiet your mind and attune yourself to the subtle energies surrounding you. Through practices like energy healing – such as Reiki or crystal healing – you can channel and balance cosmic energy within your body, promoting overall well-being. This concept invites you to explore a deeper connection with the cosmos, providing insights into your own spiritual journey and a harmonious existence.

On this journey, you will discover how embracing cosmic energy offers more than just a glimpse into the interconnectedness of all things; it provides a pathway to empowerment and purpose. So, are you ready to delve deeper into the wonders of cosmic energy and discover how it can enrich your life? The opportunity awaits, promising a rich experience that will leave you wanting to explore the boundless potential within.

# 2

# FOUNDATIONS OF NEW AGE THOUGHT

## Origins of New Age Spirituality

Embarking on the fascinating journey of New Age spirituality is akin to setting foot on a path deeply entrenched in historical and cultural influences. This transformative movement finds its roots in the mid-20th century, a period marked by an upsurge in curiosity and spiritual exploration. A collective yearning for liberation from traditional religious structures propelled individuals to blend ancient and modern spiritual elements, crafting a personalized, holistic approach to spirituality that resonated with their innermost aspirations.

The foundations of New Age practices draw profound inspiration from Eastern philosophies, notably Hinduism, Buddhism, and Taoism. These ancient traditions lay emphasis on interconnectedness, mindfulness, and the pursuit of inner peace. In adopting practices such as meditation and yoga, individuals found transformative gateways to spiritual enlightenment and self-discovery. Simultaneously, the infusion of Western mysticism, entwined with elements of the occult, alchemy, and esoteric traditions, added a layer of mystery and exploration to the burgeoning New Age movement.

As New Age spirituality gained momentum, it blossomed into a melting pot of beliefs, assimilating influences from Native American, Celtic, and other indigenous spiritual traditions. Central to New Age thought was a profound reverence for nature and a deep acknowledgment of the sacredness inherent in all living things. The movement drew inspiration from the ancient wisdom of various cultures, synthesizing their wisdom into a harmonious blend that resonated deeply with seekers on this transformative spiritual journey.

The counterculture movements of the 1960s and 1970s played an instrumental role in shaping the contours of New Age spirituality. Fueled by a rejection of mainstream norms, the embrace of psychedelics, and a quest for higher consciousness, the counterculture provided fertile ground for the expansion of the New Age movement. Visionaries within the movement sought to transcend societal constraints, envisioning a world characterized by harmony and spiritual interconnectedness.

In essence, New Age spirituality emerges as a vibrant tapestry of influences, weaving threads from the spiritual traditions of both East and West, indigenous cultures, and the transformative ideals of the counterculture. This eclectic blend creates a dynamic and ever-evolving spiritual landscape, inviting individuals to explore, question, and connect with ancient wisdom woven into the fabric of this fascinating movement.

Now, let's delve into the transformative potential inherent in harnessing the energies cultivated by New Age spirituality. At its core, this spiritual journey offers individuals a pathway to profound personal enhancement. The infusion of Eastern philosophies, with their emphasis on mindfulness and interconnectedness, provides tools for navigating the complexities of modern life. Practices such as meditation and yoga, drawn from these traditions, become powerful means to cultivate inner peace, reduce stress, and enhance overall well-being.

The adoption of Western mysticism within New Age practices introduces a sense of mystery and exploration. Individuals exploring these facets often find a deep connection to symbols, rituals,

and hidden knowledge, unlocking a rich kaleidoscope of insights and self-discovery. The integration of indigenous spiritual traditions further amplifies the transformative potential, fostering a profound connection to nature and a heightened awareness of the sacred in everyday life.

The counterculture's influence infuses New Age spirituality with a rebellious spirit, encouraging individuals to question societal norms and explore alternative paths to personal and collective growth. The embrace of psychedelics, for example, becomes a tool for expanding consciousness and gaining deeper insights into the nature of reality. This, coupled with the quest for higher consciousness, becomes a catalyst for personal transformation, opening doors to new perspectives and a more spiritually connected existence.

Furthermore, New Age spirituality not only weaves together a diverse tapestry of influences but also offers a transformative journey for those willing to explore its depths. By harnessing the energies embedded in its practices, individuals can enhance their lives on multiple levels – physically, mentally, emotionally, and spiritually. The holistic approach of New Age spirituality beckons seekers to delve into the richness of these traditions, unlocking the potential for profound self-discovery, personal growth, and a harmonious connection with the energies that shape the fabric of existence. Are you ready to embark on this transformative journey and unveil the boundless possibilities that await within the embrace of New Age spirituality?

Embarking on the profound exploration of New Age philosophy opens the doors to a comprehensive understanding of its key principles, each contributing to a holistic worldview that resonates with seekers on a deeply spiritual level. At the core of this transformative philosophy lies a celebration of global spiritual wisdom, encouraging individuals to embark on a journey that transcends cultural boundaries, fostering a unique path within the interconnected tapestry of human spirituality.

In the intricate fusion of global influences that form New Age spirituality, Eastern philosophies play a pivotal role. Drawing from the wellsprings of Hinduism, Buddhism, and Taoism, these traditions contribute fundamental concepts that serve as invaluable tools for self-discovery and spiritual growth. Practices such as meditation, karma, and interconnectedness become guiding stars, illuminating the path toward inner peace, self-realization, and a profound connection with the cosmic currents.

Indigenous traditions, deeply ingrained in New Age thought, provide a grounding force. The Native American reverence for nature and the Celtic celebration of natural cycles underscore the movement's commitment to environmental consciousness and the sanctity of the natural world. These influences not only connect practitioners to the earth but also weave a sense of sacredness into the fabric of daily existence, fostering a harmonious relationship with the interconnected web of life.

The integration of ancient mystical and esoteric Western traditions further enriches New Age spirituality. Hermeticism and alchemy, with their hidden knowledge and symbolic depth, create

a distinctive synthesis within the movement. This synthesis defines New Age spirituality, infusing it with profound symbolism and facilitating spiritual transformation through the exploration of hidden truths.

The counterculture movements of the 1960s and 1970s, marked by ideals of personal freedom, self-expression, and spiritual exploration, resonate deeply within New Age thought. These movements become catalysts for seekers to break free from societal norms, fostering an environment that encourages individuality and the pursuit of higher consciousness. The embrace of alternative healing practices, rooted in diverse cultural traditions like Ayurveda, Traditional Chinese Medicine, and indigenous healing methods, further reinforces a holistic approach to well-being.

At the heart of New Age philosophy, fundamental principles intertwine to create a vibrant spiritual understanding. Interconnectedness stands as a cornerstone, emphasizing the intricate links between all living things, contributing to a harmonious cosmic tapestry. Consciousness becomes another vital thread, exploring individual awareness as a pathway connecting us to the broader fabric of cosmic existence. This exploration encourages a journey toward higher states of consciousness, where seekers can expand their awareness and align with the universal flow of energy.

Central to New Age philosophy is the pillar of personal transformation. This principle empowers individuals not only to evolve personally but also to contribute to the collective evolution of humanity. Through self-reflection, spiritual practices, and a commitment to growth, individuals embark on a transformative journey that leads to a more harmonious and balanced existence.

Now, let's explore how these foundational principles intersect with the profound concept of cosmic energy. In the New Age perspective, cosmic energy transcends the abstract; it is a dynamic force flowing through the interconnected web of existence. This vital life force, believed to connect all living things to the universal consciousness, takes center stage for seekers within the New Age movement. Practices such as meditation and energy healing become portals through which individuals attune themselves to cosmic energy, seeking to enhance interconnectedness, elevate consciousness, and catalyze profound personal transformation.

## Key Principles of New Age Philosophy

This exploration of New Age philosophy unveils not only a rich network of global influences but also a transformative journey that invites individuals to align with profound principles, connecting with the cosmic dance of life. As you delve into this tapestry of spiritual exploration, may the wisdom embedded in these principles guide you toward a deeper understanding of yourself, your connection to the universe, and the boundless potential for personal and collective transformation that awaits within the embrace of New Age spirituality.

Embarking on a profound exploration of cosmic energy within the expansive realm of New Age philosophy invites us to unravel the intricate dance between this universal force and the human experience.

To truly grasp the significance of cosmic energy, we must delve into its essence – a concept that represents the very life force permeating every facet of existence. It serves as an invisible thread, seamlessly transcending physical boundaries and intricately connecting all living things to the vast tapestry of the cosmos.

This universal presence of cosmic energy extends beyond the abstract; it becomes a poignant invitation to explore the interconnected rhythm of existence. Within this grand symphony of the universe, individuals are offered a profound opportunity to cultivate a deep sense of unity, purpose, and transcendence. The recognition of cosmic energy as the invisible force binding us to the cosmic connection becomes the catalyst for a transformative journey, unveiling the boundless potential within the universal currents that flow through the very fabric of our being.

In the New Age philosophy, cosmic energy is not a distant or abstract concept; it is the omnipresent, dynamic force infusing every facet of our lives. This universal life force, often regarded as the guiding light of the cosmic dance, illuminates the interconnectedness woven into the very fabric of existence. It serves as a constant reminder of our integral role in the cosmic symphony, encouraging us to attune ourselves to its rhythms and harmonize with the cosmic currents.

As we contemplate the interaction of cosmic energy with the human experience within New Age spirituality, we embark on a profound journey of attunement. The conscious alignment with this universal flow becomes a key practice, fostering a harmonious resonance with the cosmic currents that permeate the essence of our being.

## The Universe and Cosmic Energy

Energy healing modalities within the New Age worldview, such as Reiki and crystal healing, are revered as sacred pathways to channel and balance cosmic energy. These practices become tangible expressions of our connection to the cosmic forces, promoting holistic well-being on physical, emotional, and spiritual levels. The wisdom embedded in the belief of cosmic energy extending beyond the physical realm prompts a mindful and intentional engagement with its subtle influences on the nuances of our existence.

In the New Age perspective, cosmic energy isn't confined to the boundaries of the physical; it gracefully extends into the realms of emotion, thought, and spirit. Embracing cosmic energy becomes an acknowledgment of its subtle influence on the multidimensional aspects of our being. This recognition prompts individuals to engage consciously with these energetic currents, unlocking the potential for elevated states of consciousness, expanded awareness, and a profound sense of interconnectedness.

We find ourselves at the threshold of a profound understanding of our interconnected place in the cosmic dance. This transformative journey unfolds through the profound interaction between cosmic energy and the human experience. By consciously aligning with universal currents, individuals open themselves to boundless possibilities intricately woven into the tapestry of existence. The forthcoming chapter promises a deeper dive into the nature of cosmic energy, unraveling its mysteries and revealing its role as a wise guide shaping the expansive landscape of New Age spirituality. Get ready to embark on an enriching journey, guided by the profound wisdom of cosmic energy, where the threads of existence lead us toward profound self-discovery and connection.

As we conclude our exploration into the foundational principles of New Age thought, we stand on the precipice of a profound understanding of cosmic energy. This universal force extends a heartfelt invitation, urging us to embark on a transformative journey into the heart of existence. Here, the threads of our being are not mere strands but intricately woven into a tapestry of interconnected wonder, unveiling the harmonious dance between the individual and the cosmos.

The culmination of our exploration sets the stage for a deeper dive into the nature of cosmic energy—a journey promising to unravel its mysteries and illuminate its role as a wise guide in shaping the vast landscape of New Age spirituality. Within the forthcoming chapter, we will navigate the cosmic currents, exploring the profound intricacies of this universal force that serves as a beacon for seekers on their spiritual quest. This cosmic energy, like a guiding light, illuminates the path toward self-discovery and connection, inviting individuals to weave their unique threads into the fabric of the cosmic symphony.

Prepare to embark on this enriching journey guided by the profound wisdom of cosmic energy, where the threads of existence lead us toward a tapestry of not only self-discovery but also a deeper connection with the vast rhythms of the universe. As we unveil the mysteries within the heart of cosmic energy, the chapters that follow will unfurl new dimensions of understanding, beckoning us to explore the boundless possibilities that lie within the interconnected dance of existence. May this journey be a source of inspiration, wisdom, and transformative insights as we navigate the cosmic landscape of New Age spirituality.

# 3

# UNDERSTANDING COSMIC ENERGY

## Nature of Cosmic Energy

In the tapestry of New Age spirituality, we now turn our gaze inward, exploring the enigmatic realm of cosmic energy in this second chapter of our journey. As we navigate the intricate layers

of existence, our focus shifts to unraveling the profound mysteries woven into the very fabric of our being—the cosmic energy that connects us to the vast symphony of the cosmos.

In the previous chapter, we glimpsed the transformative journey sparked by the interplay between cosmic energy and the human experience. Now, our exploration takes on a more introspective hue, inviting us to contemplate the essence of cosmic energy itself. This omnipresent force, an age-old beacon for seekers, beckons us to attune ourselves to its subtle vibrations and the universal currents that course through the cosmos.

This chapter serves as a guide through the rich landscape of cosmic energy, inviting readers to embark on an insightful expedition. As we peel back the layers of understanding, we unveil the profound significance of cosmic energy, a force intricately involved in shaping the very foundations of New Age spirituality. Our exploration is not just about facts; it's an invitation to immerse ourselves in the wisdom that cosmic energy carries.

Together, we will delve into the nuances of this universal force, exploring its multifaceted role in guiding us toward self-discovery, fostering connections, and harmonizing our existence within the expansive cosmic tapestry. As the pages unfold, we invite you to join us on this intellectual and spiritual journey, embracing the boundless possibilities that emerge within the mysterious dance of cosmic energy. This chapter is more than a continuation—it's an opportunity to deepen our understanding and forge a meaningful connection with the cosmic currents that flow through the very essence of our being.

Within a nuanced exploration of cosmic energy, we find ourselves drawn into the intricate tapestry of its characteristics and qualities. To grasp the essence of this universal force, we must delve beyond its abstract concept and discern the specific attributes that shape its influence across diverse world philosophies.

One prominent characteristic of cosmic energy lies in its inherent interconnectedness, a thread woven through Eastern philosophies such as Hinduism, Buddhism, and Taoism. In Hindu cosmology, the concept of Prana signifies the life force that permeates the universe, connecting all living entities. Similarly, in Buddhism, the understanding of energy or "Chi" emphasizes the interconnected nature of existence, where the ebb and flow of energy influence every aspect of life. Taoist philosophy, with its emphasis on the Tao, underscores the idea of a pervasive energy that unifies all things in a harmonious dance.

Another quality of cosmic energy manifests in its transformative nature, aligning with the principle of impermanence found in various philosophies. In the teachings of Buddhism, the concept of Anicca highlights the transient nature of all things, mirroring the ever-changing currents of cosmic energy. Similarly, the Taoist principle of Wu Wei encourages individuals to flow with the natural transformations, reflecting the dynamic essence inherent in cosmic energy.

The universal principle of balance and harmony is intricately tied to cosmic energy, resonating across cultures. In Ancient Chinese philosophy, the concept of Yin and Yang symbolizes the interplay of opposites, embodying the balance necessary for cosmic harmony. This echoes in the Ayurvedic traditions of India, where the understanding of Prana and Apana emphasizes the equilibrium of vital energies for overall well-being.

Cosmic energy also reflects a profound intelligence, akin to the Greek concept of Logos or the cosmic order. In Hermeticism, an esoteric tradition with roots in ancient Egypt, the principle of Correspondence suggests a harmony between the macrocosm (the universe) and the microcosm (individuals). This cosmic intelligence guides seekers toward aligning with the grand design of existence.

As we unravel the characteristics of cosmic energy, these examples illustrate its diverse facets, revealing a force that transcends cultural and philosophical boundaries. In the pages that follow, we will continue our exploration, examining how these qualities shape the landscape of New Age spirituality, offering insights into the profound nature of cosmic energy and its impact on the human experience.

As we venture deeper into the intricate tapestry of cosmic energy, let us broaden our perspective by considering the insights of various New Age thinkers who have contemplated the essence of this universal force. Their diverse viewpoints contribute to a richer understanding of cosmic energy, offering unique lenses through which we can explore its characteristics.

One prevalent perspective comes from renowned spiritual teacher Eckhart Tolle, who emphasizes the transformative power of presence and awareness. According to Tolle, cosmic energy is not merely an abstract force but a living, vibrant intelligence that becomes accessible through heightened consciousness. Through practices like mindfulness and presence, individuals can attune themselves to the subtle currents of this cosmic energy, facilitating personal transformation and a deeper connection to the universal flow.

Deepak Chopra, a prominent figure in holistic wellness, approaches cosmic energy through the lens of quantum healing. For Chopra, the body is a dynamic expression of cosmic energy, and by aligning with the principles of quantum physics, individuals can tap into the healing potential of this energy. Quantum healing practices, including meditation and visualization, become pathways for harnessing cosmic energy to promote physical and spiritual well-being.

A more metaphysical perspective is offered by Alice Bailey, an influential writer in esotericism. Bailey's teachings delve into the idea of a cosmic etheric plane—a realm of subtle energies that underlies the material world. In her framework, cosmic energy is the animating force that infuses this etheric plane, influencing the evolution of consciousness and fostering spiritual growth.

Dolores Cannon, a pioneer in past-life regression and hypnotherapy, provides an intriguing viewpoint on cosmic energy. Through her work, Cannon explored the concept of

multidimensional realities and the existence of higher vibrational frequencies. According to her, cosmic energy serves as a bridge between these dimensions, influencing human experiences and facilitating soul evolution.

These perspectives from New Age thinkers add depth to our exploration of cosmic energy, showcasing the multifaceted nature of this universal force. As we synthesize these insights with the characteristics we've uncovered from various world philosophies, a more comprehensive picture emerges. In the upcoming sections, we will continue our journey, weaving together these diverse threads to gain a holistic understanding of cosmic energy and its profound impact on the human experience within the framework of New Age spirituality.

## Recognizing Cosmic Energy

The practice of recognizing cosmic energy invites us to integrate awareness seamlessly into our everyday lives. This guide, devoid of chapters, is a continuous exploration—a tangible roadmap for those seeking a genuine connection with the universal forces that shape our reality.

In the pursuit of recognizing cosmic energy, the foundation lies in cultivating mindfulness and presence. Practical techniques such as meditation, conscious breathing exercises, and grounding practices become accessible tools for heightening awareness. By being fully present in the moment, individuals open themselves to the subtle vibrations of the cosmic dance, laying the groundwork for sensing cosmic energy in the midst of daily life.

The art of perceiving and interacting with energy fields forms the next step in recognizing cosmic energy. Drawing inspiration from traditions like Reiki and Qi Gong, we demystify the process of sensing energy. Practical exercises guide individuals in developing sensitivity to energy flows, fostering a tangible connection with cosmic forces. Recognizing cosmic energy transforms from an abstract concept into a skill that can be honed and integrated into daily routines.

Nature, as a beacon of cosmic connection, becomes our mentor in this continuous exploration. Spending time in natural surroundings, practicing forest bathing, and attuning ourselves to the Earth's rhythm become transformative practices. Through experiential exercises, individuals learn to recognize cosmic energy as it manifests in the natural world, infusing their everyday lives with a sense of interconnected wonder.

Unlocking the door to cosmic recognition involves tapping into intuitive insights and inner wisdom. Trusting and enhancing innate intuition becomes the focus in this continuous journey. By aligning decisions with inner guidance, individuals begin to sense the subtle influence of cosmic energy in their daily choices. This fosters a harmonious connection with the universal currents that guide us, bringing cosmic awareness into the tapestry of our daily existence.

We stand at the threshold of a transformative journey—an exploration empowering individuals to recognize, sense, and connect with cosmic energy seamlessly woven into the ebb and flow of everyday life. This guide is not a mere intellectual exercise; it's an invitation to discover the boundless possibilities unfolding within the interconnected dance of cosmic energy.

Starting on the journey of attuning yourself to cosmic energy is an exploration that goes beyond mere exercises. It's a continuous practice that seamlessly integrates into your daily life, gradually opening the gateway to a heightened awareness of the cosmic forces that intricately weave through the tapestry of existence.

Begin your journey with the simplicity of mindful breathing. Find a quiet space to sit comfortably, allowing the rhythm of your breath to guide you into the present moment. As you inhale, envision drawing in the positive cosmic energy that surrounds you, and as you exhale, release any tension or negativity. Through this rhythmic practice, you cultivate a profound connection with the subtle vibrations of the cosmic dance, discovering the boundless possibilities within each breath.

Grounding exercises serve as a foundational step in this transformative journey. Stand barefoot on natural ground, whether it's the earth, grass, or sand. Visualize roots extending from your feet into the rich soil beneath, firmly anchoring you in the present moment. As you draw up the Earth's grounding energy through these roots, you establish a harmonious connection with the vitality of the planet, recognizing your integral role in the cosmic symphony.

Energy awareness meditation guides you through an exploration of your inner landscape. Visualize each part of your body being filled with a gentle, glowing energy, gradually expanding this awareness until your entire being is enveloped in a cosmic energy field. This meditation not only deepens your connection with the cosmic forces within but also fosters an understanding of the intricate dance between your individual energy and the vast cosmic tapestry.

Nature, with its inherent connection to cosmic energy, becomes a guiding companion on your journey. Immerse yourself in natural surroundings, whether it be a serene park, a majestic forest, or the rhythmic waves of the sea. Absorb the elements—feel the warmth of the sun, the caress of the wind, and the textures beneath your fingertips. Engage your senses in this cosmic ballet, allowing the natural world to impart its wisdom and energy, inviting you to harmonize with the broader cosmic rhythm.

As you delve into intuitive insights journaling, you open the door to your inner wisdom. Before moments of meditation or quiet reflection, seek insights related to cosmic energy. Record any impressions, thoughts, or images that surface, creating a tangible record of your evolving connection with the cosmic forces. Periodically revisiting these entries unveils patterns, offering insights into the dynamic interplay between your intuitive self and the vast cosmic energies.

Crystal meditation, featuring stones resonant with cosmic energy like clear quartz or amethyst, acts as a bridge between the tangible and the ethereal. Hold the crystal in your hand, feeling its

energy radiate through you. Envision the crystal as a conduit for cosmic vibrations, attuning your own energy to the universal currents. Through this practice, you learn to synchronize your individual energy with the cosmic dance, realizing that you are an integral part of the grand symphony.

As you integrate these practices into your daily life, you pave the way for a profound attunement to cosmic energy. This journey is not just about exercises; it's an immersive experience that leads you to recognize the intricate connection between your individual self and the vast cosmic forces that shape the very essence of existence. The cosmic dance becomes a reflection of your own journey—a journey toward self-discovery, connection, and an enriched understanding of the boundless possibilities embedded within the cosmic energy that surrounds you.

## Cosmic Energy and the Self

In the sacred tapestry of existence, the relationship between cosmic energy and individual consciousness unfolds as a profound dance, weaving threads of wisdom and insight into the very fabric of our being. At the heart of this cosmic connection lies the understanding that individual consciousness is not a separate entity but a harmonious note in the grand symphony of the universe.

Individual consciousness, like a unique melody, resonates with the cosmic energy that permeates all of creation. It is an expression of the universal consciousness that flows through the vast cosmic currents. In the quiet moments of self-reflection and meditation, individuals can attune themselves to this cosmic dance, recognizing the interconnectedness between their own consciousness and the boundless energy that courses through the cosmos.

As seekers delve into the exploration of cosmic energy, they come to realize that consciousness is not confined to the individual self but is a thread interwoven with the collective consciousness of the universe. This realization transforms the understanding of the self from a separate entity to an integral part of the cosmic whole. In this realization, individual consciousness expands, transcending the boundaries of ego and embracing a more expansive awareness of interconnected existence.

Meditative practices serve as gateways to this profound connection. As individuals quiet the fluctuations of the mind and turn their awareness inward, they create a space for the cosmic energy to flow seamlessly into their consciousness. In this stillness, the boundaries between individual and cosmic consciousness begin to dissolve, fostering a sense of unity and oneness.

The cosmic dance influences individual consciousness in subtle yet transformative ways. The heightened awareness cultivated through practices like meditation allows individuals to navigate the intricate energies that shape their thoughts, emotions, and perceptions. As cosmic energy intertwines with individual consciousness, a deepened understanding of the self

emerges—an understanding that transcends the limitations of the physical body and taps into the eternal stream of universal wisdom.

Moreover, the relationship between cosmic energy and individual consciousness extends beyond the confines of the physical realm. It encompasses the realms of emotion, thought, and spirit, influencing the very essence of what it means to be alive. Embracing cosmic energy involves recognizing its subtle influence on the nuances of our existence, prompting a mindful and intentional engagement with these energetic currents.

In the cosmic dance of consciousness, individuals become co-creators, actively participating in the evolution of their own awareness and contributing to the broader unfolding of universal consciousness. This dance invites individuals to explore the boundless potential within the cosmic currents, fostering a sense of purpose, interconnectedness, and transcendence.

As seekers embrace the interplay between cosmic energy and individual consciousness, they embark on a journey of self-discovery and spiritual growth. The dance becomes a dialogue—an exchange of energies where the individual learns from the cosmic wisdom and, in turn, contributes their unique vibrations to the universal chorus. It is a symbiotic relationship, a sacred communion that transcends the limitations of language and thought, guiding individuals toward the profound realization that they are not merely observers but active participants in the cosmic dance of consciousness.

Within the vast cosmic dance, the concept of the higher self emerges as a luminous facet, intricately connected to the flowing currents of cosmic energy. The higher self is not merely a distant aspiration but a dynamic expression of our most elevated and enlightened potential—a reflection of the divine within us that resonates with the cosmic symphony.

As seekers traverse the landscapes of self-discovery and cosmic connection, they encounter the notion of the higher self as a guiding light, beckoning them toward a deeper understanding of their purpose and essence. It is the eternal aspect of our being, untouched by the transient fluctuations of everyday life, and intimately entwined with the boundless energy that pervades the cosmos.

In the dance between cosmic energy and the higher self, individuals come to recognize that the higher self is not a separate entity but an integral part of the cosmic whole. It is a timeless essence that transcends the limitations of individual consciousness, resonating with the universal consciousness that threads through the fabric of existence. The higher self becomes a conduit for the cosmic energies, channeling their transformative power into the tapestry of our lives.

Meditative practices, such as connecting with the breath and attuning to the cosmic energy, serve as pathways to commune with the higher self. In these contemplative moments, seekers can experience a harmonious alignment, as the higher self becomes a bridge between individual consciousness and the expansive realms of universal wisdom. It is in these moments

of connection that individuals may receive insights, intuitions, and profound guidance from the higher self, which acts as a compass on their spiritual journey.

The higher self, infused with cosmic energy, is not bound by the constraints of the physical realm. It transcends the limitations of ego and material existence, inviting individuals to perceive life from a heightened perspective. As seekers align with the cosmic currents, the higher self guides them toward a more profound understanding of their purpose, illuminating the path of spiritual evolution and self-realization.

Furthermore, the dance between cosmic energy and the higher self is a dynamic interplay that unfolds in the realms of consciousness, unveiling the latent potentials and capacities within each individual. The higher self serves as a reservoir of divine wisdom, encouraging seekers to tap into their innate creativity, intuition, and compassion. As individuals attune themselves to the higher self through the cosmic energies, they embark on a transformative journey, unlocking the dormant aspects of their being and integrating them into their daily lives.

The dance with the higher self also involves surrender—a surrender to the wisdom of the cosmos and an openness to receive the guidance and blessings it bestows. In this surrender, individuals release the illusions of separateness and control, allowing the higher self to guide them with a wisdom that transcends the intellect and aligns with the eternal truths of the universe.

In conclusion, the dance between cosmic energy and the higher self is an exquisite choreography, inviting individuals to embrace the fullness of their divine nature. As seekers explore the realms of cosmic connection, they not only attune to the cosmic energies that surround them but also align with the radiant essence of their higher self. This union becomes a transformative journey—a journey into the depths of one's being, guided by the wisdom of the higher self and illuminated by the eternal radiance of cosmic energy.

# 4

# MEDITATION AND COSMIC ENERGY

## Meditation Basics

Meditation, a timeless and transformative practice, unveils the art of cultivating heightened awareness, presence, and focus. It is a sacred journey inward, an exploration of the profound landscapes within the mind, heart, and spirit. Across diverse cultures and spiritual traditions, meditation stands as a universal gateway to self-discovery and inner peace.

At its essence, meditation is a deliberate act of turning attention inward, away from the external distractions of the world, to forge a deep connection with one's inner self. This intentional

process often involves the nurturing of mindfulness—a state of non-judgmental awareness of the present moment. Through a rich tapestry of techniques, individuals seek to quiet the ceaseless chatter of the mind, rise above the ordinary fluctuations of thought, and access a profound stillness that resides within.

Meditation, far from a rigid practice, takes on a myriad of forms, offering flexibility to accommodate the diverse needs and preferences of those who engage in it. Whether focusing on the rhythmic breath, immersing in visual imagery, chanting sacred mantras, or mindfully observing thoughts and sensations, meditation caters to a spectrum of approaches, providing a personalized journey into the realms of inner exploration.

This ancient practice transcends the boundaries of specific religious or spiritual traditions, welcoming individuals from all backgrounds to its universal embrace. Rooted in Eastern philosophies like Buddhism and Hinduism, seamlessly integrated into Western mindfulness practices, and echoed in indigenous spiritual traditions, meditation stands as a tool for

self-discovery, inner peace, and a profound connection with the subtle energies woven into the fabric of the cosmos.

As seekers engage in the meditative process, they embark on a transformative odyssey, inviting a quiet revolution within themselves. The potency of meditation extends beyond the tranquility and mental clarity it offers; it becomes a conduit for a deepened connection with cosmic energy. This universal force, subtle and pervasive, intertwines with the very essence of our being. In the upcoming chapters, we will journey together into the symbiotic relationship between meditation and cosmic energy, exploring how this sacred practice serves as a vessel for attunement to the cosmic currents flowing through the vast tapestry of existence. Prepare to embrace the wisdom that arises from the stillness within, as meditation becomes a portal to the cosmic dance of the universe.

As we navigate the profound journey of meditation, we uncover a spectrum of gentle techniques designed to guide beginners into the sacred space of inner exploration. Meditation, at its heart, is an intentional practice that invites us to turn inward, cultivating a heightened awareness and connection with the boundless energies that weave through the cosmos.

Breath Awareness Meditation becomes our first companion on this journey. Find a quiet, comfortable space, settle into a relaxed posture, and gently close your eyes. Allow your attention to rest on the natural rhythm of your breath. Inhale and exhale with a gentle awareness, observing the breath as it flows effortlessly. As thoughts arise, acknowledge them without judgment and tenderly bring your focus back to the soothing cadence of your breath. This practice not only anchors us in the present moment but also unveils the tranquility that resides within.

Guided Visualization emerges as a pathway into the realm of meditation. Picture a serene landscape in your mind—a tranquil forest, a sunlit meadow, or the gentle waves of an ocean. Engage your senses in this inner sanctuary, feeling the softness of the grass, hearing the rustle

of leaves, and sensing the warmth of the sun. Guided visualization serves as a gentle introduction, allowing us to explore the landscapes of our inner world and discover the profound stillness within.

In the rhythmic repetition of Mantra Meditation , we find a harmonious dance between sound and spirit. Choose a simple and meaningful mantra—a word or phrase that resonates with your essence. Sit comfortably, close your eyes, and allow the mantra to reverberate within you. As you repeat it, feel the resonance deepening, creating a sacred space for contemplation. This practice becomes a gentle melody, guiding us into the heart of stillness and inviting a profound connection with the cosmic energies that surround us.

Loving-Kindness Meditation becomes a balm for the soul. Sit in a comfortable position, and with each breath, extend feelings of love and kindness. Begin by directing these sentiments towards yourself and gradually expand them to embrace loved ones, acquaintances, and even those with whom you may find challenges. This practice becomes a beacon of compassion, fostering a heart-centered awareness and revealing the interconnected threads that bind us to the vast tapestry of existence.

Try a Body Scan Meditation, a journey of self-discovery through mindful attention to your body. Find a comfortable position, close your eyes, and bring your awareness to different parts of your body, starting from your toes and gradually moving upward. Notice sensations, tensions, or relaxations in each area. This practice becomes a mindful exploration, revealing the intricate connection between body and mind and inviting a profound sense of relaxation.

As you embrace these foundational techniques, let your meditation practice unfold organically. Approach it with patience and compassion, allowing the gentle currents of cosmic energy to guide you deeper into the sanctuary of your own being. In the quietude of meditation, may you discover not only the tranquility that resides within but also the interconnected dance between your essence and the cosmic symphony that envelops us all.

Embarking on the sacred practice of meditation unveils a profound journey into the depths of self-discovery and spiritual illumination. At its essence, meditation serves as a conduit through which individuals can attune themselves to the subtle energies that permeate the vast cosmos, including the potent force known as cosmic energy.

Within the meditative state, we intentionally cultivate heightened awareness and presence. By quieting the incessant chatter of the mind and immersing ourselves in the serenity of the present moment, we create a receptive inner space. This stillness allows us to become finely attuned to the subtle vibrations of cosmic energy flowing through the vast tapestry of existence.

Meditation offers a unique opportunity to align individual consciousness with the universal consciousness, facilitating a connection to the boundless reservoir of cosmic energy surrounding us. Through focused intention and deep introspection, practitioners can learn to harness this cosmic energy, nourishing their inner being and elevating their spiritual journey.

A pivotal aspect of meditation lies in expanding consciousness. Delving into the meditative state enables us to transcend the limitations of the ego, accessing higher levels of awareness. This expanded consciousness not only opens our perception to the interconnectedness of all things but also reveals our integral role in the cosmic dance of existence.

Furthermore, meditation promotes a profound sense of inner harmony and balance, creating an optimal environment for the seamless flow of cosmic energy. By cultivating states of inner peace and tranquility, practitioners align themselves with the natural rhythms of the universe, tapping into the transformative power inherent in cosmic energy.

Meditation also nurtures a heightened sensitivity to subtle energy currents within the body. Practices such as breath awareness and body scanning foster an acute awareness of the subtle sensations that arise within. This heightened sensitivity allows individuals to perceive the delicate movements of cosmic energy as it gracefully flows through their being, establishing a deeper connection with the universal life force.

In essence, meditation serves as a powerful and transformative tool for harnessing cosmic energy. Through the cultivation of inner stillness, expansion of consciousness, and fostering of inner harmony, individuals create an optimal environment for the flow of cosmic energy within themselves. Regular meditation practice becomes a sacred ritual, enabling practitioners to tap into the boundless potential of cosmic energy, nourishing their souls, awakening higher potentials, and harmonizing with the divine rhythm of the universe.

## Visualization Techniques

In the sacred realm of meditation, visualization practice emerges as a tapestry of profound imagination and inner exploration. This transformative technique invites practitioners to paint vibrant mental landscapes, weaving together the threads of intention, imagery, and emotion.

Picture, if you will, a tranquil sanctuary within your mind—a place of serene beauty or personal significance. As you close your eyes and embark on this inner journey, the external world fades away, and you find yourself immersed in the rich hues of your imagination. Here, the mind's eye becomes a canvas upon which you paint intricate scenes, symbols, or scenarios.

This visual odyssey is more than a mere exercise; it is a deliberate act of creation. In the gentle act of visualizing, you breathe life into the chosen focal point, infusing it with details that engage the senses. The mind becomes an artist, meticulously crafting the colors, textures, sounds, and scents associated with the envisioned imagery.

As you delve deeper into the tapestry of your imagination, the practice transcends the boundaries of the physical world. The chosen focal point may be a sanctuary of nature, a cherished memory, or a symbolic representation of your aspirations. The act of envisioning is

not confined to the visual; it encompasses a multisensory experience that stirs emotions and fosters a profound connection with the inner self.

In this sacred space of visualization, distractions fade into the background, and a gentle current of focus guides the mind. The chosen imagery becomes a portal to a realm where time loses its grip, and the present moment expands into a sanctuary of inner stillness.

The beauty of visualization lies in its versatility. For some, it serves as a balm for stress, inviting a deep sense of relaxation. Others wield this practice as a tool for concentration, training the mind to hold steady in the face of life's distractions. It is a method that transcends the boundaries of the tangible, allowing for exploration, healing, and even manifestation.

Imagine the ripple effect of this practice extending beyond the meditation session—its influence seeping into the fabric of daily life. The clarity of intention cultivated through visualization becomes a guiding light, illuminating the path toward the manifestation of aspirations and dreams.

In the realm of spirituality, visualization becomes a sacred dance with the divine, a means of connecting with higher states of consciousness or seeking guidance from the spiritual realm. The richness of this practice lies not only in the images created but in the emotions stirred, the connections forged, and the transformative potential it holds.

As you navigate the landscapes of your mind through visualization, remember that this is more than a creative endeavor; it is an intimate conversation with the depths of your being. Each brushstroke of imagination, each nuance of emotion, contributes to the masterpiece of

self-discovery unfolding within the canvas of your consciousness. In this sacred act of envisioning, the mind becomes a conduit for the limitless possibilities that lie within the realm of inner exploration.

In the realm of meditation, the practice of visualization unfolds as a sacred dance with the cosmic energies that weave through the tapestry of existence. As you embark on this inner journey, envision your mind as a radiant beacon, drawing upon the energies of the cosmos to enrich and elevate your meditative experience.

Begin by settling into a comfortable position, allowing the cares of the external world to gently fade away. Close your eyes, and with each breath, create a sacred space within. Imagine this inner sanctuary as a tranquil haven, bathed in the soft glow of cosmic energy.

Now, let your mind's eye conjure a focal point—an image or symbol that resonates with the energy you seek to connect with. It could be a celestial body, a cosmic spiral, or an ethereal light—something that symbolizes the vast, interconnected dance of the universe. As you visualize, infuse this chosen focal point with a luminous energy, feeling its vibrancy resonate within.

As you deepen into the meditation, sense the energy of the cosmos flowing around and through you. Envision the currents of cosmic energy as gentle waves, gracefully caressing the contours of your being. Feel the subtle vibrations, recognizing that you are an integral part of this cosmic dance.

In this visual exploration, imagine your breath as a rhythmic dance with the cosmic currents. With each inhalation, draw in the cosmic energy, allowing it to permeate every cell of your being. As you exhale, release any tension or negativity, letting it dissolve into the expansive cosmos. Feel the reciprocity between your breath and the cosmic energy, a harmonious exchange that deepens your connection with the universal life force.

As you continue visualizing, expand your awareness to encompass the entire cosmos. Envision the galaxies, stars, and celestial bodies as interconnected nodes within a vast web of energy. Sense your own energy aligning and resonating with this cosmic symphony, creating a harmonious melody that reverberates through the cosmos.

Now, bring your focus back to the inner sanctuary you've created. Feel the cosmic energy infusing every aspect of your being—mind, body, and spirit. Visualize yourself as a radiant being, a conduit for the cosmic energies to flow freely. Embrace the interconnected dance, recognizing that the energy you channel is an integral thread in the cosmic tapestry.

In this sacred practice of visualization, you are not merely an observer but an active participant in the cosmic ballet. As you deepen your connection with the cosmic energies, allow a sense of gratitude to permeate your being. Gratitude for the boundless energy that sustains and connects us all, fostering a deep sense of unity within the grand cosmic design.

As you gradually conclude this visualization, carry the awareness of cosmic energy with you. Recognize its omnipresence in your daily life, inviting you to align with the harmonious currents that weave through the cosmos. Through the practice of visualization, you have opened a portal to a deeper connection with cosmic energy—a connection that transcends the boundaries of time and space, inviting you to become a conscious participant in the cosmic dance of existence.

For those new to the enchanting realm of visualization within meditation, let us embark on a gentle journey that invites cosmic energy into the sanctuary of your consciousness. Find a comfortable space, free from distractions, and allow this practice to unfold with grace and ease.

1. Grounding and Centering:

Begin by taking a few deep breaths to ground yourself in the present moment. Feel the support of the Earth beneath you and visualize roots extending from your body, anchoring you securely to the ground. As you breathe in, draw in the nurturing energy of the Earth; as you exhale, release any tension or worries.

1. Inner Sanctuary:

Close your eyes and imagine a tranquil sanctuary within your mind—a place that feels safe, serene, and filled with gentle light. This could be a meadow, a beach, a forest, or any location that resonates with tranquility. Allow the details of this inner sanctuary to unfold with each breath.

1. Celestial Focal Point:

In the center of your inner sanctuary, visualize a celestial focal point—an image or symbol representing cosmic energy. It could be a radiant star, a cosmic spiral, or a shimmering light. Picture this focal point as a source of divine energy, emitting a soft and harmonious glow.

1. Cosmic Breath:

As you breathe deeply, imagine inhaling not just air but the very essence of cosmic energy. With each inhalation, sense the celestial energy filling your lungs and permeating every cell of your being. As you exhale, release any tension, allowing it to dissolve into the cosmic expanse.

1. Connection with Celestial Bodies:

Expand your awareness beyond your inner sanctuary to the cosmic vastness. Visualize the galaxies, stars, and celestial bodies dancing in a harmonious symphony. Feel your own energy aligning and resonating with the cosmic dance, recognizing the interconnectedness of all things.

1. Energy Exchange:

Envision a continuous flow of energy between your being and the cosmos. As you breathe, sense the reciprocity between your breath and the cosmic currents. Visualize your breath as a rhythmic dance, a gentle exchange that deepens your connection with the universal life force.

1. Radiant Being:

Visualize yourself as a radiant being, infused with the luminous energy of the cosmos. See your entire being illuminated with a celestial light, transcending the boundaries of the physical body. Feel the oneness with the cosmic energy, recognizing yourself as an integral part of the grand cosmic design.

1. Gratitude and Completion:

As you gently conclude this visualization, express gratitude for the cosmic energy that flows through you. Feel a deep sense of unity and interconnectedness with the cosmos. Carry this awareness with you as you gradually return to the present moment, knowing that you have touched the cosmic energies that dance within and around you.

This step-by-step guide is an invitation to beginners, guiding you to explore the cosmic dimensions of your inner world. As you integrate this practice into your meditation journey, may it awaken a profound connection with the cosmic energy that weaves through the tapestry of existence.

## Chakra Meditation

The concept of chakras, often regarded as energetic centers within the human body, has ancient roots and finds its origins in the spiritual traditions of India. The term "chakra" is derived from Sanskrit, meaning "wheel" or "disk." These spinning wheels of energy are thought to be vital points where various aspects of our consciousness and life force converge.

The earliest references to the chakra system can be traced back to ancient Indian texts known as the Vedas, particularly the Rigveda and Upanishads, dating as far back as 1500 BCE. The Upanishads, in particular, delve into the subtle anatomy of the human body, describing the flow of energy through nadis (energy channels) and the convergence of these energies at specific points—the chakras.

In the yogic tradition, the concept of chakras gained prominence as a part of Kundalini Yoga, a practice aimed at awakening the dormant spiritual energy (Kundalini) believed to reside at the base of the spine. The chakra system became intricately linked to the path of spiritual awakening, providing a map for understanding the interplay between physical, mental, and spiritual dimensions.

The seven main chakras, each associated with specific qualities and functions, are aligned along the spine from the base to the crown. These are:

1. Root Chakra (Muladhara): Located at the base of the spine, it is associated with grounding, stability, and survival instincts.

2. Sacral Chakra (Swadhisthana): Found in the pelvic area, it relates to creativity, passion, and emotional well-being.

3. Solar Plexus Chakra (Manipura): Situated in the upper abdomen, it governs personal power, confidence, and self-esteem.

4. Heart Chakra (Anahata): Located in the center of the chest,

it is associated with love, compassion, and emotional balance.

5. Throat Chakra (Vishuddha): Positioned at the throat, it governs communication, self-expression, and truth.

6. Third Eye Chakra (Ajna): Situated between the eyebrows, it relates to intuition, insight, and spiritual awareness.

7. Crown Chakra (Sahasrara): Found at the top of the head, it represents higher consciousness, spiritual connection, and transcendence.

While the concept of chakras originated in ancient Indian spiritual practices, it has transcended cultural boundaries and is now embraced and adapted by various spiritual traditions and New Age practices worldwide. The understanding of chakras serves as a valuable tool for those exploring the intricate connection between the physical body and the subtle energies that animate our existence.

Starting the exploration of the chakra system invites us into the rich tapestry of our own energetic landscape—a landscape intricately connected to the cosmic energies that weave through the universe. The chakras, those spinning wheels of energy positioned along the central axis of our being, offer a profound framework for understanding the interplay between our physical, emotional, and spiritual dimensions.

In the embrace of the chakra system, we find a sacred map that guides us through the various energetic centers within our body. Each chakra serves as a portal, a gateway through which cosmic energy flows, nourishing and harmonizing the intricate dance of our existence. The ancient wisdom embedded in the chakra system, originating from the spiritual traditions of India, resonates across time and culture, inviting us to explore the profound connection between our inner world and the cosmic energies that permeate the universe.

As we journey through the chakras, we embark on a pilgrimage of self-discovery, delving into the unique qualities and attributes associated with each energetic center. These spinning vortices of energy not only reflect our physical well-being but also serve as windows into the deeper realms of consciousness and spirituality. The chakra system becomes a bridge, connecting the microcosm of our individual experience to the macrocosm of the cosmos.

In this exploration, we discover that each chakra resonates with specific cosmic frequencies, inviting us to attune ourselves to the universal rhythms that echo through the fabric of reality. As we engage with the chakra system, we open ourselves to the subtle currents of cosmic energy, allowing them to flow through the channels of our being. The chakras become conduits, harmonizing our inner energies with the expansive dance of the cosmos.

This journey into the chakra system is an invitation to awaken the dormant potentials within, to align ourselves with the cosmic forces that guide our existence. Through this sacred framework, we navigate the realms of physical vitality, emotional balance, mental clarity, and spiritual transcendence. The chakras, like celestial gateways, beckon us to experience the profound interconnection between our individual journey and the cosmic symphony of creation. May this exploration be a source of inspiration, guiding you toward a deeper understanding of yourself within the vast expanse of cosmic energy.

Guided meditations offer a beautiful pathway to align and balance the chakras, creating a harmonious flow of energy within our being. As we embark on these meditative journeys, let us immerse ourselves in practices that invite cosmic energy to dance through the subtle realms of our chakra system.

1. Root Chakra Meditation (Muladhara):

Begin by finding a comfortable seated position. Close your eyes and take a few deep breaths to ground yourself. Visualize a vibrant red light at the base of your spine, representing the root chakra. As you breathe, imagine the energy expanding and creating a sense of stability and connection to the Earth. Affirmations like "I am grounded and secure" can deepen the meditation. Spend a few minutes in this visualization, feeling the energy flowing freely.

1. Sacral Chakra Meditation (Swadhisthana):

Sit comfortably and bring your attention to the lower abdomen. Envision an orange glow in this area, symbolizing the sacral chakra. With each breath, allow the energy to swirl and cleanse, fostering creativity and emotional well-being. Affirmations such as "I embrace pleasure and abundance" can enhance the experience. Dive into the warmth of the orange light, letting it radiate through your entire pelvic region.

1. Solar Plexus Chakra Meditation (Manipura):

Find a quiet space and sit with a straight spine. Focus on the area above your navel, envisioning a radiant yellow light—the solar plexus chakra. Inhale deeply, allowing the energy to expand and empower you. Affirmations like "I am confident and in control" resonate with the solar plexus. Feel the warmth and brightness of the yellow light infusing your core, bringing a sense of empowerment and self-assurance.

1. Heart Chakra Meditation (Anahata):

Sit in a comfortable position, placing your hands over your heart. Close your eyes and visualize a lush green light at the center of your chest—the heart chakra. Breathe deeply, allowing the energy to expand with each breath. Focus on feelings of love, compassion, and forgiveness.

Affirmations like "I am open to love and compassion" can amplify the heart-centered experience. Imagine the green light enveloping you in a sphere of unconditional love.

1. Throat Chakra Meditation (Vishuddha):

Sit with an erect spine and bring attention to your throat. Picture a soothing blue light, representing the throat chakra. Inhale deeply, allowing the blue energy to swirl and clear communication pathways. Affirmations such as "I express myself with clarity and authenticity" resonate with the throat chakra. Feel the gentle vibrations of the blue light resonating in your throat, promoting truthful self-expression.

1. Third Eye Chakra Meditation (Ajna):

Find a quiet space and sit in a comfortable position. Focus on the space between your eyebrows, visualizing an indigo light—the third eye chakra. Inhale and exhale, allowing the indigo energy to expand your intuition and inner wisdom. Affirmations like "I trust my inner guidance" can deepen the meditation. Feel the clarity and insight of the indigo light opening your inner vision.

1. Crown Chakra Meditation (Sahasrara):

Sit in a comfortable and upright position. Direct your attention to the top of your head, visualizing a luminous violet or white light—the crown chakra. Inhale deeply, allowing the energy to ascend, connecting you to higher states of consciousness. Affirmations like "I am connected to the divine" can elevate the experience. Feel the expansive and transcendent qualities of the violet or white light infusing your being.

These simple guided meditations provide a gentle yet profound way to align and balance your chakras, fostering a harmonious flow of cosmic energy within. Regular practice can deepen your connection to the subtle energies that dance through the chakra system, inviting a sense of balance, vitality, and spiritual well-being into your life. May these meditative journeys guide you toward a deeper understanding of your own cosmic dance.

# 5

# Cosmic Energy Healing Practices

## Introduction to Energy Healing

In the gentle embrace of cosmic energy, we find the gentle currents that weave the fabric of our existence, offering profound avenues for healing and restoration. As we step into this chapter, we embark on a journey through the realms of cosmic energy healing—a journey that beckons us to uncover the timeless wisdom of practices designed to harmonize our energies with the cosmic dance.

Cosmic energy healing practices stand as ageless bridges between the universal life force and our well-being, providing gateways to balance and vitality across the layers of our being. Rooted in an understanding of the interconnected rhythms of cosmic energies, these practices become sacred rituals to recalibrate the subtle energies that shape our physical, emotional, and spiritual dimensions.

Within these pages, we shall unravel diverse cosmic energy healing modalities, each a distinct expression of the boundless energies flowing through the cosmos. From the gentle touch of Reiki and the crystalline resonance of crystal healing to the vibrational harmonies of sound therapy and the subtle shifts of energy attunements, these practices emerge as conduits, guiding us toward healing and transformation. Nurtured by the wisdom passed through generations and inspired by the cosmic symphony, these modalities illuminate the way to wholeness.

But why do these practices matter? They matter because they invite us to tap into the expansive reservoirs of cosmic energy surrounding us, offering profound tools for self-healing and empowerment. By aligning with cosmic energy, we create a channel to an infinite wellspring of

wisdom and vitality, transcending the confines of the physical realm. Our exploration into cosmic energy healing practices becomes a pilgrimage of self-discovery, where the cosmic currents gracefully support our quest for holistic well-being.

Prepare to immerse yourself in the realms of energy healing—a sacred space where ancient wisdom and cosmic forces converge to bring healing, balance, and transformation into our lives. Through these practices, we unfold the art of harmonizing with the cosmic energies that gracefully dance through the universe, providing a sanctuary for renewal and restoration. May this exploration be a radiant beacon on your path to cosmic energy healing, guiding you toward a deeper understanding of the cosmic currents that intertwine with the essence of your being.

In the gentle ebb and flow of the cosmic dance, the utilization of cosmic energy for healing emerges as a time-honored practice, offering a profound journey towards balance and well-being. This ancient approach acknowledges cosmic energy not only as a life force but also as a transformative power that can be consciously directed to foster healing on physical, emotional, and spiritual levels.

At its core, the process involves attuning oneself to the cosmic energies that gracefully weave through the universe, recognizing their interconnected dance with our own energies. Here, the practitioner assumes the role of a conduit, channeling the harmonious currents of cosmic energy to create a healing resonance within the individual's energy field.

One primary avenue through which cosmic energy is employed for healing is Reiki—a Japanese form of energy healing. In this practice, the practitioner becomes a vessel, allowing the universal life force to flow through them and into the recipient. The gentle laying of hands facilitates relaxation, balance, and holistic healing as cosmic energy courses through the energetic pathways.

Crystal healing stands as another modality that leverages cosmic energy for therapeutic purposes. Crystals, revered as carriers of vibrational frequencies, amplify and transmit cosmic energies. Placing crystals on or around the body facilitates the absorption of cosmic energy, aligning it with the individual's energy centers and promoting harmonization and rejuvenation.

Sound therapy, too, provides an avenue for utilizing cosmic energy in healing. Instruments like singing bowls or tuning forks, when played intentionally, create vibrational frequencies that resonate with cosmic energies. This resonance influences the energy fields of the recipient, inducing relaxation, releasing tension, and fostering a sense of energetic alignment.

In essence, the practice of using cosmic energy for healing involves a conscious collaboration with the universal life force. Practitioners, armed with knowledge and attunement, become orchestrators of this cosmic symphony, allowing healing energies to gracefully flow where needed. Whether through hands-on healing, crystal work, or vibrational therapies, the intention remains to restore the natural flow of cosmic energy within the individual, promoting a state of equilibrium and vitality.

As we delve into the realms of cosmic energy healing practices, we open ourselves to the transformative potential within the expansive cosmic symphony. This utilization of cosmic energy becomes a sacred art—a dance of healing that harmonizes the individual with the universal currents, revealing the profound interconnectedness that exists between the cosmos and our own being.

## Self-Healing Techniques

Beginning this journey of energy healing unveils a rich tapestry of modalities, each offering a unique approach to harnessing the subtle forces that influence our well-being. From ancient practices rooted in Eastern traditions to modern methodologies, these modalities provide pathways for individuals to tap into their innate healing potential. Let's explore some of these modalities and delve into self-healing techniques that empower individuals to cultivate a harmonious balance within.

Reiki, originating from Japan, is a widely practiced energy healing modality. The word "Reiki" translates to "universal life energy," reflecting its core philosophy. In Reiki, practitioners channel healing energy through their hands, placing them gently on or near the recipient's body. This promotes relaxation, reduces stress, and facilitates the natural flow of energy within the body. Reiki is guided by the principle that life force energy sustains our physical, emotional, and spiritual well-being.

Qi Gong, rooted in Chinese medicine and philosophy, is an ancient practice that harmonizes the body's vital energy, or "Qi." This modality combines mindful movement, breathwork, and meditation to cultivate balance and strengthen the flow of Qi. Qi Gong exercises range from gentle, flowing movements to more dynamic postures, all aimed at promoting the harmonious circulation of energy throughout the body. Practitioners often experience enhanced vitality, improved flexibility, and a sense of inner calm.

Pranic Healing, developed by Grandmaster Choa Kok Sui, is a holistic energy healing system that operates on the principle of manipulating "prana" or life energy. Practitioners use specific techniques to cleanse, energize, and balance the body's energy centers, known as chakras. By working on the energetic body, Pranic Healing addresses imbalances that may manifest as physical or emotional ailments. This modality emphasizes the importance of maintaining a healthy energy body for overall well-being.

In addition to these external modalities, individuals can engage in self-healing techniques that empower them to actively participate in their well-being journey. Mindfulness meditation, for instance, encourages awareness of the present moment, fostering a deep connection with one's inner self. This practice has been associated with reduced stress, improved mental clarity, and enhanced emotional well-being.

Breathwork, a powerful self-healing tool, involves conscious control of the breath to influence the body's physiological and energetic states. Techniques such as diaphragmatic breathing and alternate nostril breathing can help balance the nervous system, promote relaxation, and optimize the flow of life force energy.

Affirmations, another form of self-healing, involve the repetition of positive statements to shift mindset and energetic patterns. By consciously directing thoughts and intentions, individuals can cultivate a more positive and supportive internal dialogue, influencing their overall energetic state.

As we explore these diverse modalities of energy healing and self-healing techniques, it becomes evident that the intricate dance of energy within and around us holds the key to profound well-being. These practices, whether administered by external practitioners or embraced as part of personal routines, invite individuals to become active participants in their healing journey, tapping into the limitless reservoirs of cosmic energy that surround and permeate their existence.

In the expansive realm of cosmic energy, individuals can access simple yet profound techniques to actively participate in their healing journey. Rooted in the understanding of the interconnectedness between individual energy and cosmic currents, these practices invite individuals to nurture their well-being. Here are accessible techniques for self-healing with cosmic energy:

1. Conscious Breathing:

Engage in conscious breathing exercises to harmonize your energy. Practice deep diaphragmatic breathing, inhaling slowly through your nose, allowing your abdomen to expand, and exhaling gently. Visualize cosmic energy entering your body with each inhalation, revitalizing and cleansing your energetic being.

1. Visualization Meditation:

Utilize the power of visualization to direct cosmic energy for healing. Close your eyes and envision a cascade of vibrant energy descending upon you. Visualize this energy flowing through every cell, illuminating and purifying your entire being. Focus on specific areas of your body that may require healing or envision a blanket of healing light enveloping you.

1. Energy Center Activation:

Connect with your chakras by placing your hands over each energy center. Starting from the base of the spine, move your hands upward, pausing at each chakra. As you hover over each energy center, visualize cosmic energy swirling and balancing the chakra. This technique enhances the vitality of your energy centers, promoting overall well-being.

1. Affirmations and Intention Setting:

Harness the power of positive affirmations and intentional thoughts to influence your energetic state. Create personalized affirmations that resonate with your healing goals, such as

"I am vibrant and filled with cosmic healing energy." Repeat these affirmations regularly, allowing them to permeate your consciousness and align your energy with healing frequencies.

1. Grounding Practices:

Ground yourself by connecting with the Earth's energy. Spend time in nature, walking barefoot on natural surfaces, or simply sitting with your back against a tree. Visualize roots extending from your body into the Earth, anchoring you and allowing any excess energy to flow into the ground.

1. Crystal Healing:

Integrate the energy of crystals into your self-healing routine. Select crystals known for their healing properties, such as amethyst for spiritual healing or rose quartz for emotional

well-being. Place the chosen crystal on the corresponding energy center or hold it in your hands during meditation to amplify the flow of cosmic energy.

1. Sound Healing:

Explore the transformative effects of sound vibrations on your energy field. Listen to soothing sounds, such as Tibetan singing bowls or crystal bowls, to resonate with cosmic frequencies.

Alternatively, experiment with toning or chanting simple mantras to attune your energy to healing vibrations.

1. Energetic Cleansing Rituals:

Incorporate cleansing rituals into your routine to release stagnant energy. A simple salt bath or smudging with sage can help purify your energetic field, allowing cosmic energy to flow freely.

Visualize any accumulated negativity or tension dissipating into the cleansing elements.

As you engage in these self-healing techniques, remember that consistency and intention amplify their effectiveness. Embrace the journey of self-discovery and healing, trusting in the inherent connection between your energy and the boundless cosmic forces that surround you.

As you embark on your cosmic energy journey, consider starting with accessible practices that resonate with the essence of your being. Begin with mindful breathwork, a simple yet powerful technique that requires no special equipment. Find a quiet space, connect with your breath, and let its rhythmic flow become a conduit for the universal life force. Inhale deeply, exhale slowly, and feel the subtle currents of cosmic energy weaving through your being.

Guided meditation offers a gentle introduction to cosmic connection. Explore online resources or meditation apps that cater to beginners. These sessions often guide you through visualizations, affirmations, and grounding techniques, fostering a harmonious resonance with the cosmic energies that surround you. Allow yourself the freedom to explore and discover which guided meditations align most authentically with your energy and intentions.

Nature, with its boundless energies, becomes a sacred space for grounding and rejuvenation. Spend time outdoors, whether in a local park or a natural setting. Take mindful walks, feel the

Earth beneath your feet, and let the elements inspire a sense of connection. Nature serves as a powerful ally in aligning your energy with the Earth's energies, facilitating a harmonious exchange that resonates with the cosmic dance.

Embarking on these accessible practices is a step toward weaving your own tapestry of connection with the cosmic energies that permeate the universe. Approach the journey with curiosity, openness, and a sense of joy as you explore the profound depths of your own energetic landscape.

As you deepen your connection with cosmic energy, you may find that your newfound awareness can extend beyond personal transformation. Cosmic energy, when harnessed with intention and compassion, has the potential to become a healing force for others. Whether through gentle touch, guided meditations, or simply sharing the uplifting vibrations cultivated within, your connection to cosmic energy can ripple outward, offering solace and healing to those around you.

Consider this journey not only as a personal exploration but also as a pathway to becoming a conduit of cosmic healing energies. As you attune to the cosmic currents, you may discover the profound impact your aligned energy can have on others. The healing power of cosmic energy is not confined to individual experiences but has the capacity to create a collective tapestry of well-being, fostering harmony, balance, and interconnectedness within the broader human experience.

As you continue to explore, remember that the tapestry you weave is a unique expression of your connection with cosmic energy. Embrace the transformative potential of these practices, not only for personal growth but also for the beautiful ripple effect they can create, contributing to the collective healing energy of the universe.

## Healing Others with Cosmic Energy

on the journey of sharing healing energy with others is a profound and responsible endeavor. As you explore this path, it's essential to consider ethical principles that honor the well-being and autonomy of those receiving the healing energies. Here are key considerations to guide your practice:

1. Respect for Consent:

Always seek explicit consent before sharing healing energy with others. Respect their autonomy and personal boundaries, ensuring they feel comfortable and open to receiving the energy. Communicate transparently about the nature of the practice and its potential effects.

1. Integrity and Authenticity:

Approach the sharing of healing energy with sincerity and authenticity. Maintain integrity in your intentions, ensuring that your energy comes from a place of genuine compassion and a

desire to support others on their journey. Authenticity fosters trust and enhances the effectiveness of the energetic exchange.

1. Empowerment and Collaboration:

Cultivate an empowering approach by viewing the sharing of healing energy as a collaborative process. Encourage individuals to actively participate in their own healing journey and emphasize the role of cosmic energy as a catalyst for their innate healing abilities. Foster a sense of empowerment rather than creating dependency.

1. Awareness of Energetic Boundaries:

Develop a keen awareness of energetic boundaries. Respect the energetic autonomy of both yourself and the individuals you are assisting. Be mindful not to impose your energy on others but rather create a space for harmonious exchange where healing energies can flow freely.

Techniques for Sharing Healing Energy:

1. Intentional Touch:

If appropriate and with consent, incorporate gentle touch as a channel for sharing healing energy. This can be done through techniques like Reiki, where the practitioner lightly places their hands on or near specific areas of the recipient's body. Intentional touch can enhance the energetic connection and promote a sense of comfort.

1. Guided Energetic Meditations:

Share healing energy through guided meditations that focus on energetic alignment and balance. Utilize visualizations and affirmations to guide individuals in attuning to cosmic energy. This approach encourages active participation, allowing them to be co-creators in their healing process.

1. Energy Infusion through Objects:

Infuse objects with healing energy and offer them as supportive tools. Crystals, for example, are believed to hold and amplify energy. Sharing energetically charged crystals or other objects allows individuals to carry the healing energy with them, fostering a continuous connection.

1. Distance Healing:

Explore distance healing techniques where you send healing energy to individuals remotely. This can be achieved through focused intention, visualization, and practices such as absent healing. Always seek consent and maintain a compassionate connection, even when physical proximity is not possible.

Approach the sharing of healing energy with humility, recognizing that each individual's journey is unique. By navigating with ethical considerations and employing various techniques, you contribute to a collective tapestry of well-being and support within the interconnected web of cosmic energy.

Closing the door on our exploration of Cosmic Energy Healing Practices, we find ourselves at the threshold of a profound understanding of harnessing cosmic energy for the well-being of ourselves and others. As you embark on your journey into the healing arts, remember that ethical considerations and a deep sense of responsibility are the pillars upon which a harmonious energy healing practice stands.

Begin this transformative journey by nurturing a profound self-awareness. Through practices like meditation and mindfulness, attune yourself to the subtle nuances of your own energetic presence. Understand your energy patterns and tendencies, establishing a solid foundation for ethical and intentional energy sharing.

Trust in the wisdom of your intuition as you engage in energy healing sessions. Your inner guidance acts as a compass, offering valuable insights into the needs of the recipient and the flow of energy. Pay attention to these subtle cues, allowing your intuition to inform your actions and create a more attuned and responsive healing experience.

Continual learning and training are essential in the evolving field of energy healing. Stay informed about various techniques, perspectives, and ethical considerations. This commitment to ongoing education enhances your skills, deepens your understanding, and ensures that your practice aligns with the highest ethical standards.

Maintain clear and healthy boundaries within your energy healing practice. Clearly communicate the scope and nature of your services, ensuring a shared understanding between you and the recipient. Establishing boundaries safeguards the integrity of the healing space and contributes to a safe and respectful environment.

Incorporate grounding practices into your routine to anchor yourself and maintain energetic balance. Techniques such as walking in nature, visualization, or working with grounding crystals can help you stay centered and connected to the Earth's stabilizing energies. Grounding is vital for both your well-being and the effectiveness of energy sharing.

Prioritize self-care to replenish your own energy and prevent burnout. Engage in activities that bring you joy, relaxation, and rejuvenation. Nurturing your well-being ensures that you approach energy healing from a place of abundance, enhancing your capacity to support others.

Foster open and transparent communication with those you assist in energy healing. Encourage them to share their experiences, feelings, and any sensations they may encounter during sessions. This collaborative approach creates a supportive space for mutual understanding and growth.

Connect with experienced energy healers or mentors who can offer guidance, supervision, and insights. Learning from seasoned practitioners provides valuable perspectives and helps you navigate challenging aspects of energy healing with wisdom and discernment.

Engage in regular self-reflection to assess your experiences and refine your practice. Explore the impact of your energy sharing on both yourself and the recipients. Honest self-reflection contributes to your personal and professional growth, allowing you to adapt and enhance your skills over time.

As you conclude this chapter, remember that cultivating sensitivity and responsibility in energy healing is a continual journey. Approach your practice with humility, curiosity, and a commitment to the well-being of both yourself and those you have the privilege to support on their healing path.

# 6

## MANIFESTING WITH COSMIC ENERGY

### The Law of Attraction

Embarking on the exploration of Manifesting with Cosmic Energy invites you into the transformative realm of intentional creation. In this chapter, we will delve into the profound principles of the Law of Attraction, unraveling how cosmic energy intricately shapes our reality. Prepare to uncover the art of consciously crafting your life, creating abundance, and surmounting obstacles through the dynamic interplay of cosmic energies.

At the core of manifesting lies the Law of Attraction, a fundamental principle that suggests similar energies attract one another. It proposes that the energies we emit—whether in the form of thoughts, emotions, or intentions—act as magnetic forces, drawing similar energies into our lives. As we unravel the threads of this universal law, we'll explore how cosmic energy serves as a potent catalyst, amplifying our manifesting abilities.

Creating abundance, both material and spiritual, becomes a harmonious dance with cosmic energy. We will navigate the intricate tapestry of intention-setting, visualizations, and energy alignment, unraveling the secrets to manifesting prosperity and fulfillment. From attracting opportunities to cultivating a mindset of abundance, this chapter will guide you in harnessing cosmic energy to manifest a life rich in both substance and meaning.

Moreover, as we venture deeper into the realm of manifestation, we will confront and transcend obstacles that may hinder the realization of our desires. Cosmic energy, with its boundless potential, becomes a guiding force in overcoming challenges, transforming adversity into stepping stones toward our aspirations. Through the fusion of intention, cosmic alignment,

and resilience, we'll explore how manifesting with cosmic energy transcends the mere pursuit of goals—it becomes a profound journey of personal growth and empowerment.

So, get ready to unlock the secrets of the Law of Attraction, explore the art of abundance creation, and navigate the cosmic currents to overcome obstacles on your path. Manifesting with Cosmic Energy invites you to become an active participant in shaping the narrative of your life, harnessing the expansive energies of the cosmos to manifest your deepest desires and aspirations.

The Law of Attraction is a fundamental principle rooted in the idea that like attracts like. This universal concept posits that the energies individuals emit through their thoughts, emotions, and intentions act as magnetic forces, attracting corresponding energies into their lives. In essence, the focus on positive or negative thoughts can influence and shape one's experiences.

The origins of the Law of Attraction can be traced back to ancient wisdom traditions, where the principle of correspondence, as expressed in Hermeticism, highlighted the interconnectedness of thoughts and external reality. The 19th-century New Thought movement further explored the influence of thought on health, happiness, and success. Notable figures such as Phineas Quimby and William Walker Atkinson contributed to the foundational understanding of the Law of Attraction during this period.

The term "Law of Attraction" gained prominence in the early 20th century, particularly through the writings of William Walker Atkinson, a key figure in the New Thought movement. In the 21st century, the concept experienced a resurgence with the popularity of books like "The Secret" by Rhonda Byrne, which presented the Law of Attraction as a central principle for achieving personal and professional success.

While interpretations of the Law of Attraction may vary, the core idea remains consistent: the profound influence of one's thoughts and intentions in shaping their experiences and reality. This concept has become a focal point in self-help and personal development discussions, sparking exploration into the dynamic relationship between individual consciousness and the unfolding of life experiences.

In the expansive landscape of cosmic energy, the Law of Attraction operates as a dynamic force, intricately woven into the interconnected web of universal energies that saturate the cosmos. It posits that the thoughts and intentions emanating from individuals are not isolated occurrences but integral components of the cosmic dance. Here, cosmic energy serves as the conduit through which the Law of Attraction materializes.

# HARNESSING COSMIC ENERGY

Cosmic energy, often acknowledged as the universal life force, is perceived to traverse through all living entities, establishing a profound connection between individuals and the expansive tapestry of the cosmos. Within the context of the Law of Attraction, cosmic energy assumes the role of a carrier wave, transporting the thoughts and intentions of individuals into the cosmic

expanse. The vibrational frequencies of these mental emissions resonate with the cosmic energies, initiating a magnetic pull that draws corresponding energies and experiences back into the individual's life.

Picture cosmic energy as the foundational current in an immense ocean, with individual thoughts acting as ripples on its surface. The Law of Attraction, in this cosmic framework, proposes that the energy released into the cosmic ocean creates ripples that extend outward, interfacing with the universal currents and eventually returning with experiences aligned with the emitted energy.

Moreover, within the cosmic energy paradigm, the Law of Attraction underscores the principles of unity and interconnectedness. It suggests that the thoughts and intentions of individuals not only shape their personal experiences but also contribute to the collective energy of the cosmos. The cosmic dance, therefore, mirrors the collective vibrations emitted by all living beings, creating a symphony that can either harmonize or discord based on the prevailing energies.

In summary, grasping the intricacies of the Law of Attraction within the domain of cosmic energy invites individuals to recognize their role as co-creators in the cosmic dance. It advocates for mindfulness regarding the energies one projects into the universe, acknowledging the profound impact these energies can have on personal experiences and the overarching cosmic tapestry. By aligning thoughts and intentions with the positive, harmonious frequencies of cosmic energy, individuals may augment their ability to attract experiences resonant with the elevated vibrations of the cosmic dance.

## Creating Abundance

Within the intricate dance of cosmic energy, the concept of abundance takes center stage, offering a pathway to manifesting prosperity in various aspects of life. Abundance, in the context of cosmic energy, involves cultivating a mindset and vibrational frequency that attracts positive experiences, opportunities, and resources. Here's an in-depth exploration of how to create abundance through the harmonious interplay of intention, cosmic energy, and the Law of Attraction:

1. Clarity and Specificity:

Begin by gaining clarity on the specific areas of life where you seek abundance. Whether it's financial wealth, meaningful relationships, career success, or overall well-being, articulate your desires with precision. Specific intentions create a clear roadmap for cosmic energy to align with and amplify.

1. Aligning Intentions with Values:

Ensure that your intentions for abundance align with your core values and aspirations. When your desires resonate with your authentic self, the vibrational harmony intensifies, making it more conducive for cosmic energy to respond.

1. Positive Affirmations for Abundance:

Craft positive affirmations specifically geared towards attracting abundance. These affirmations should reflect a mindset of plenty and prosperity. For instance, affirmations like "I am a magnet for abundance" or "I attract prosperity effortlessly" infuse your consciousness with the energy of abundance.

1. Visualization for Abundance:

Engage in regular visualization practices where you vividly imagine yourself living a life of abundance. Picture the details of financial success, fulfilling relationships, and overall prosperity. Visualization serves as a powerful tool to align your energy with the abundant frequencies of the cosmic field.

1. Emotional Resonance with Abundance:

Infuse positive emotions into your thoughts about abundance. Feel the joy, gratitude, and fulfillment associated with living an abundant life. Emotions serve as a magnetic force that enhances the vibrational match between your energy and the abundance you wish to attract.

1. Gratitude for Current Abundance:

Acknowledge and express gratitude for the abundance already present in your life. Focusing on existing blessings creates a positive energy flow, attracting more abundance into your experience. Gratitude amplifies the cosmic resonance of abundance.

1. Generosity and Sharing:

Embrace the principle of giving as a way to receive. Acts of generosity and sharing create a positive energetic flow that aligns with the abundance principle. By circulating positive energy, you open yourself to receiving more in return.

1. Empowerment Through Action:

Take inspired action aligned with your intentions. Abundance often follows purposeful and aligned effort. Cosmic energy responds to the initiative and commitment you demonstrate in realizing your aspirations.

1. Affirmation of Worthiness:

Cultivate a deep sense of worthiness to receive abundance. Recognize your inherent value and deserving nature. When you believe in your worthiness, you emit a powerful frequency that resonates with the cosmic abundance available to you.

By integrating these practices into your daily life, you actively participate in the co-creation of abundance. The cosmic energy field becomes a responsive and dynamic force, magnetizing experiences that align with your intentions for prosperity and fulfillment.

The intricate dance between cosmic energy and the Law of Attraction is a fascinating exploration of how the universe responds to our intentions and vibrations. Originating from the concept that like attracts like, the Law of Attraction posits that the energies we emit—whether through thoughts, emotions, or intentions—draw corresponding energies from the vast cosmic field.

Cosmic energy, as the pervasive force that interconnects all aspects of the universe, serves as the conduit through which the Law of Attraction operates. At its core, this law implies that the vibrational frequency of our thoughts and feelings influences the energetic tapestry of the cosmos. When we consciously align our intentions with positive emotions, we set in motion a harmonious resonance with the vibrational frequency of abundance within the cosmic energy field.

The role of cosmic energy in the Law of Attraction is akin to that of a receptive medium. It registers and amplifies the vibrational imprints of our desires, thoughts, and emotions. As we project a focused intention for abundance into the cosmic realm, this energy becomes a transmitter, carrying our unique vibrational signature across the interconnected web of the universe.

The interconnected nature of cosmic energy ensures that our intentions send ripples through the fabric of existence. This interconnectedness allows our desires to reach and resonate with the broader cosmic field, creating a subtle yet powerful influence on the quantum possibilities within the universe.

In the co-creative process between cosmic energy and the Law of Attraction, our consciousness plays a vital role. By consciously directing our thoughts and intentions towards abundance, we engage in a dynamic exchange with cosmic forces. This conscious focus serves as a guiding force, informing the cosmic field of our desires and initiating a responsive dance between our intentions and the universal energies.

Furthermore, within the quantum field—a realm where possibilities exist as potential states—cosmic energy is intertwined. As we focus our thoughts on abundance, we interact with this quantum field, influencing the probabilities of events and outcomes. This intricate dance between our consciousness, cosmic energy, and the quantum field shapes the manifestation of abundance in our reality.

The timeless influence of cosmic energy implies that our intentions have a continuous resonance within the cosmic continuum. Beyond the constraints of time and space, the vibrational imprints of our desires persist, creating an enduring magnetic pull towards abundance throughout the journey of our lives.

In essence, cosmic energy acts as both the canvas upon which the Law of Attraction paints our intentions and the dynamic medium through which our conscious focus shapes the energetic

landscape of our reality. This collaboration invites us to recognize the profound interplay between our consciousness and the cosmic forces, offering a deeper understanding of how abundance manifests within the tapestry of cosmic energy.

Cultivating an abundance mindset is a transformative journey that involves aligning your thoughts, emotions, and intentions with the vibrational frequency of cosmic energy. By adopting positive affirmations and engaging in mindful practices, you can foster a mindset that attracts abundance into your life.

Affirmations:

1. Magnetism of Abundance: Affirm that you are a magnet for abundance, and it flows effortlessly into your life.

2. Aligned Thoughts: Recognize that your thoughts are aligned with the prosperity of the universe, creating a harmonious vibrational match.

3. Birthright of Abundance: Affirm that abundance is your birthright, and you welcome it with open arms as a natural aspect of your existence.

4. Trust in Infinite Abundance: Cultivate trust in the infinite abundance of the universe to provide for you in all aspects of your life.

5. Continuous Growth: Acknowledge that every day, in every way, you are becoming more and more abundant, embracing a mindset of continuous growth.

6. Release Scarcity Thinking: Declare your intention to release all scarcity thinking, allowing yourself to embrace the wealth of possibilities around you.

7. Gratitude as Key: Recognize that gratitude is the key to unlocking the flow of abundance in your life, fostering appreciation for what you have.

8. Openness to Receive: Affirm that you are open to receiving all the wealth and prosperity the universe has for you, embracing the concept of receptivity.

9. Abundance in Life: Declare that your life is filled with an abundance of love, joy, and financial prosperity, acknowledging abundance on multiple levels.

10. Co-Creation with the Universe: Affirm that you are a co-creator with the universe, manifesting abundance effortlessly through your thoughts and actions.

Practices:

1. Gratitude Journaling: Incorporate a practice of gratitude journaling into your daily routine, reflecting on and appreciating positive aspects of your life.

2. Visualization: Engage in visualization exercises where you create a vivid mental image of your desired abundance, enhancing the vibrational match with cosmic energy.

3. Daily Affirmation Ritual: Establish a daily ritual of repeating your chosen affirmations, preferably in front of a mirror, allowing positive statements to influence your subconscious mind.

4. Act As If: Embody the mindset of abundance in your actions, making decisions and choices as if you already possess the abundance you desire.

5. Generosity Practice: Cultivate a spirit of generosity by giving without expecting anything in return, fostering a positive flow of abundance.

6. Mindful Breathing: Practice conscious breathing to center yourself, inhaling positivity and exhaling negativity, creating space for abundance to manifest.

7. Release Limiting Beliefs: Identify and challenge any limiting beliefs about abundance, replacing them with empowering thoughts aligned with the limitless possibilities of the universe.

8. Affirmation Visualization: Combine affirmations with visualization during meditation, picturing corresponding images of abundance in your mind.

9. Abundance Mantra Meditation: Choose a mantra resonating with abundance and repeat it during meditation to enhance the vibrational frequency associated with prosperity.

10. Vision Board Creation: Create a vision board with images and words symbolizing your desired abundance, placing it where you can see it daily to reinforce your intentions.

Integrating these affirmations and practices into your daily routine establishes a harmonious alignment with the abundant flow of the universe, paving the way for a mindset that effortlessly attracts prosperity and fulfillment.

## Overcoming Obstacles with Cosmic Energy

These practices are intricately connected through a holistic approach that aligns the individual with cosmic energy, fostering a transformative mindset and resilience in the face of obstacles. Positive reframing serves as the foundation, encouraging a shift in perception from challenges

as setbacks to opportunities for growth. This change in mindset lays the groundwork for the subsequent practices.

Affirmations for resilience act as affirmations of one's capacity for overcoming challenges, creating a positive and empowering narrative. Visualization practices complement this by reinforcing the belief in finding creative solutions. When these practices converge, they establish a mental landscape that resonates with the abundant nature of cosmic energy.

Maintaining an abundance mindset during adversity unifies these practices, ensuring a continuous flow of opportunities and resources. Generosity amplifies this connection by creating a positive energetic exchange, opening channels for cosmic energy to respond in kind. By cultivating an attitude of gratitude, individuals harmonize with the cosmic flow, attracting more of what they appreciate.

Mindful breathing and centering practices provide a tangible and immediate connection to the present moment, creating a calm space for intuitive insights from cosmic energy. Tailored affirmations for specific obstacles infuse intention into the energy flow, addressing challenges with precision. Collaborative efforts and connection acknowledge the interconnected nature of cosmic energy, tapping into the power of synergy.

Intuitive decision-making becomes the thread that weaves these practices together, guiding individuals to align their choices with cosmic energy. This alignment allows for a seamless integration of abundance practices, transforming challenges into opportunities for growth, resilience, and a profound connection with the cosmic energy that shapes the abundant universe.

As we traverse these narratives of transformation, we uncover the timeless wisdom woven into the cosmic fabric of existence. The stories of Sarah and Michael serve as guiding constellations, illuminating the path toward intentional living and the harmonious dance with cosmic energy.

Beyond the surface, these accounts unveil the profound interconnectedness between individual aspirations and the responsive nature of cosmic energy. Sarah's resilience and Michael's

self-discovery showcase the transformative potential embedded within intentional practices. It is a reminder that, as we align our intentions with the cosmic currents, we become active participants in the co-creation of our narratives.

Now, as we stand at the intersection of inspiration and action, the question arises: How can these practices be seamlessly integrated into our daily lives? The answer lies in the gentle infusion of intention into our routines – a mindful breath before a crucial meeting, a moment of gratitude before sleep, or a conscious pause to visualize abundance amid life's hustle.

Consider the sunrise as a metaphor for this integration. In its daily ritual, the sun doesn't surge abruptly into the sky; it emerges gradually, casting a warm glow that touches every corner of the world. Similarly, integrating cosmic energy practices is not about radical upheavals but about infusing intention into the fabric of our existence, allowing it to radiate steadily, illuminating the mundane with the extraordinary.

As we embrace intentionality in our daily lives, we become custodians of our cosmic narratives, orchestrating our unique dance with the energies that shape our journey. The stories of transformation become not just anecdotes but invitations – beckoning us to infuse each day with intention, mindfulness, and the wisdom distilled from the cosmic symphony.

In the chapters that follow, we will delve deeper into the practical aspects of incorporating these practices into the ebb and flow of our daily existence. Prepare to embark on a journey where the ordinary becomes extraordinary, and the mundane transforms into a canvas for cosmic co-creation. May this journey be a source of inspiration, guiding you toward a life infused with intention, purpose, and the ever-present energy that dances through the tapestry of the cosmos.

## 7

## INTEGRATING PRACTICES INTO DAILY LIFE

As we delve into the realm of integrating cosmic energy practices into our daily lives, we open ourselves to a transformative journey that extends beyond spiritual exploration. This chapter serves as a roadmap for infusing our everyday experiences with the profound wisdom of cosmic energy. From the intimate dynamics of our relationships to the sanctity of our homes, every facet of our existence offers an opportunity to cultivate a deeper connection with the cosmic energies that surround us.

Our relationships, whether with ourselves or others, serve as fertile ground for the manifestation of cosmic energy. By infusing these connections with intention and awareness, we can elevate our interactions to a higher plane of understanding and compassion. Through conscious communication, empathy, and presence, we harness the power of cosmic energy to nurture and strengthen the bonds that unite us.

At home, where we retreat to recharge and rejuvenate, the presence of cosmic energy holds the potential to transform our living spaces into sanctuaries of peace and harmony. By creating sacred rituals, honoring the natural rhythms of the environment, and incorporating elements of mindfulness and intention into our daily routines, we invite the subtle yet profound influence of cosmic energy to permeate every corner of our homes.

Throughout this chapter, we will explore practical techniques and insights for integrating cosmic energy practices into our daily lives. From morning rituals that set the tone for the day to evening reflections that cultivate gratitude and presence, each moment offers an opportunity to align with the flow of cosmic energy and experience a deeper sense of connection and purpose.

Join me on this journey as we discover how the wisdom of cosmic energy can enrich our daily experiences, infusing every moment with meaning, vitality, and joy. Together, let us explore the infinite possibilities that arise when we embrace the transformative power of cosmic energy in our lives.

## Routine and Ritual

A routine is a series of habitual and repeated actions designed to structure daily activities. It encompasses the regular patterns and sequences that shape our daily lives, such as waking up at a specific time, engaging in exercise, preparing meals, or completing work-related tasks.

Routines provide a sense of predictability and contribute to overall well-being by establishing a structured framework for our daily activities.

In contrast, a ritual involves intentional and symbolic activities that hold personal or cultural significance. These activities often include specific gestures, words, or objects that carry a deeper meaning beyond their practical function. Rituals are commonly associated with religious or spiritual practices, ceremonies, and celebrations but can also be integrated into secular and personal contexts.

The crucial distinction lies in the intention and meaning behind these actions. While routines primarily offer structure and efficiency, rituals provide a way to connect with a deeper sense of purpose, spirituality, or personal significance. Both routines and rituals play essential roles in our lives, contributing to a sense of order, meaning, and connection with ourselves, others, and the world around us.

Establishing a routine or ritual for engaging with cosmic energy is a profound endeavor, offering a structured and consistent approach to connecting with the expansive energies that weave through the fabric of the universe. This intentional practice becomes a dedicated time and space, allowing individuals to forge a deeper connection with the subtle forces that surround us.

Consistency plays a pivotal role in working with cosmic energy. Through the regularity of a routine, individuals create a rhythm of connection, gradually attuning themselves to the cosmic energies over time. The repetition and commitment embedded in a routine become the

conduits through which the transformative potential of cosmic energies can be harnessed and woven into the tapestry of daily life.

Beyond mere repetition, routines and rituals act as anchors amidst the tumultuous pace of modern existence. They offer pockets of tranquility and reflection, serving as intentional pauses amid the chaos. These moments of stillness allow individuals to step back from the demands of daily life and reconnect with the larger rhythms of the universe, fostering inner peace, balance, and harmony.

The creation of a routine or ritual for cosmic energy engagement extends beyond a mere schedule; it is an act of self-care and commitment to spiritual growth. The dedicated space carved out for these practices becomes a sanctuary for exploration, self-awareness, and alignment with the universal energies enveloping us.

Ultimately, the significance of integrating cosmic energy practices into daily routines lies in the transformative journey it initiates. It is an odyssey towards deeper spiritual connection,

self-discovery, and a harmonious synchronization with the cosmic dance of existence.

Embracing cosmic energy in our daily lives is a transformative journey, weaving its threads into the tapestry of our routines. At its core, a routine or ritual is a set of intentional practices that cultivate a sense of rhythm, mindfulness, and connection with the cosmic energies that surround us. Let's delve into the essence of routines and rituals and explore how they can elevate our daily existence.

A routine is a sequence of activities regularly followed, providing structure and predictability to our daily lives. On the other hand, a ritual is a symbolic act or ceremony performed with specific intent, often carrying deeper meaning or spiritual significance. Both share the common thread of intentionality, creating a sacred space within the ordinary.

Creating a routine or ritual around cosmic energy practices serves as a mindful bridge between the mundane and the spiritual. It establishes a framework for consciously engaging with the energies that flow through the cosmos, grounding the ethereal in the tangible. The repetition of these practices fosters a sense of continuity, gradually infusing our daily lives with the transformative essence of cosmic energy.

Daily Practices:

1. Morning Cosmic Affirmations: Begin each day by expressing gratitude and setting positive intentions. Embrace the vast cosmic energies, inviting their guidance and influence into your daily endeavors.

2. Breathwork and Meditation: Dedicate a few moments to center yourself through conscious breathing and meditation. Connect with the universal currents, allowing their soothing presence to permeate your being.

3. Cosmic Visualization: Incorporate a brief visualization session during quiet moments. Envision yourself enveloped in shimmering cosmic energy, fostering a sense of protection and connection.

4. Lunchtime Grounding Exercise: Take a short break to step outside, connecting with nature. Feel the earth beneath your feet, absorb its energy, and open yourself to the cosmic currents that recharge your spirit.

5. Evening Reflection: Before bedtime, engage in reflective practices. Acknowledge moments of cosmic connection throughout the day, journaling your experiences to deepen your alignment with universal energies.

Weekly Practices:

1. Crystal Cleansing Ritual: Cleanse and recharge your crystals weekly, infusing them with fresh cosmic energy. Visualize the cleansing process, enhancing the metaphysical properties of your crystals.

2. Cosmic Bath Soak: Treat yourself to a cosmic-inspired bath, using Epsom salts and essential oils. Intend to cleanse and rejuvenate your energy, visualizing cosmic currents washing away stress and negativity.

3. Energy-Cleansing Space Ritual: Weekly, cleanse your living spaces energetically. Use sage or palo santo with cosmic intentions, purifying and refreshing the energy in your environment.

4. Stargazing Night: Dedicate an evening to stargazing, immersing yourself in the cosmic symphony overhead. Foster a sense of awe and connection as you contemplate the vastness of the universe.

Monthly Practices:

1. New Moon Intentions: Utilize the cosmic energy of the new moon to set intentions for the month ahead. Write down aspirations, infusing them with the potent energy of a lunar new beginning.

2. Chakra Balancing Meditation: Monthly, perform a comprehensive chakra balancing meditation. Visualize cosmic energy flowing through each chakra, cleansing and aligning these energy centers.

3. Full Moon Release Ritual: During the full moon, engage in a release ritual. Reflect on what no longer serves you, symbolically releasing old energy patterns through burning or burying written reflections.

4. Cosmic Energy Expedition: Plan a monthly outdoor activity that connects you with nature. Immerse yourself in the cosmic energies of the natural world, fostering a deep sense of unity and rejuvenation.

These practices infuse your daily, weekly, and monthly rhythms with cosmic energy, offering a harmonious blend of routine and variety to nourish your spiritual journey. They become intentional acts that bridge the earthly and the cosmic, creating a sacred dance with the energies that surround us. As you weave these practices into the fabric of your life, may you find inspiration, connection, and a profound sense of harmony with the cosmic symphony.

## Cosmic Energy and Relationships

Cultivating a connection with cosmic energy not only transforms individual lives but also radiates into relationships, creating a tapestry of positive influence. The intentional practices and rituals performed daily contribute to a heightened atmosphere of positivity and harmony, impacting interactions and fostering deeper connections.

In relationships, cosmic energy becomes a guiding force. Shared practices create shared moments, strengthening the bond and promoting a mutual understanding. Improved communication, heightened empathy, and a cosmic perspective contribute to conflict resolution, allowing challenges to be viewed as opportunities for growth.

Family dynamics are harmonized through shared cosmic rituals, grounding members in a familial cosmic narrative. In intimate partnerships, cosmic practices deepen intimacy, creating a shared language for spiritual growth. Beyond close relationships, the energy cultivated extends to social connections, influencing the collective vibe and fostering authentic connections.

As relationships are influenced by cosmic energy, they contribute to the cosmic dance, each connection becoming a unique interplay of energies within the grand symphony of the universe. Embracing cosmic energy in relationships is an invitation to co-create and dance in harmony with the universal currents that connect all of existence. May your connections be enriched, your understanding deepened, and your shared experiences become a vibrant expression of the cosmic symphony that echoes through the tapestry of life.

In the intricate dance of personal relationships, cosmic energy emerges as a transformative force, weaving threads of connection and elevating the tapestry of shared experiences. When consciously harnessed, cosmic energy becomes a silent partner, guiding relationships toward greater understanding, empathy, and harmony.

At its essence, cosmic energy serves as a unifying essence, transcending the mundane and connecting individuals on a deeper, spiritual level. Shared practices and rituals undertaken together create a sacred space where partners can delve into the core of their being, fostering

authenticity and vulnerability. This depth of connection transforms ordinary moments into opportunities for shared growth and profound understanding.

Communication, often the heartbeat of relationships, takes on a new dimension when infused with cosmic energy. The heightened awareness and mindfulness cultivated through cosmic practices enable individuals to truly listen and empathize with their partners. Words become imbued with intention, fostering a language of love, support, and encouragement.

Conflict, an inevitable part of any relationship, undergoes a metamorphosis when viewed through the lens of cosmic energy. Rather than being perceived as a source of discord, challenges become opportunities for mutual evolution. The cosmic perspective encourages partners to approach disagreements with compassion, understanding, and a shared commitment to growth.

Moreover, as cosmic energy influences personal relationships, it brings forth a sense of interconnectedness with the universal flow of existence. This awareness allows individuals to see beyond the surface and recognize the sacredness in one another. Partners become

co-creators in the cosmic dance, contributing their unique energies to the ever-expanding tapestry of life.

In the realm of personal relationships, cosmic energy acts as a silent orchestrator, guiding partners in a dance of love, understanding, and shared evolution. The journey becomes not merely a tandem exploration but a cosmic collaboration, where the energies of two individuals harmonize to create a unique and beautiful expression within the vast symphony of the universe. May your relationships be blessed with the wisdom and warmth of cosmic energy, nurturing bonds that resonate with the eternal dance of existence.

In nurturing connectivity and harmony within relationships through the embrace of cosmic energy, deliberate practices become the keystones of this transformative journey. These intentional activities not only deepen the connection with your partner but also invite a shared exploration of the boundless possibilities within the cosmic dance of existence.

Cosmic Rituals for Couples:

Establishing shared rituals infuses a sense of sacredness into daily life. Whether it's a morning meditation, an evening gratitude practice, or a weekly cosmic energy session, engaging in these rituals together creates a harmonious rhythm that aligns the energies of both partners.

Energy Bonding Exercises:

Explore exercises that focus on energy exchange and bonding. Sit facing each other in a comfortable, quiet space. Close your eyes and breathe deeply. Imagine a flow of cosmic energy between you, connecting at the heart center. As you inhale, visualize positive energy flowing from your heart to your partner's, and as you exhale, receive their energy. This practice enhances empathy and strengthens the energetic connection.

Cosmic Communication:

Elevate your communication by infusing it with cosmic awareness. Practice mindful listening and speaking, allowing the energy of your words to reflect positive intentions. Use phrases that resonate with cosmic principles, fostering an environment of love, compassion, and mutual growth.

Shared Vision Board Creation:

Collaborate on a vision board that represents your shared aspirations and cosmic journey. Include images, quotes, and symbols that hold cosmic significance for both of you. This tangible representation becomes a visual reminder of your collective cosmic path, aligning your energies toward shared goals.

Cosmic Date Nights:

Infuse your date nights with cosmic energy by choosing activities that align with your spiritual exploration. Attend workshops, engage in stargazing, practice partner yoga, or explore energy healing together. These shared experiences deepen your cosmic connection and offer opportunities for growth and joy.

Gratitude Rituals:

Establish a daily or weekly gratitude practice with your partner. Sit together and express gratitude for the cosmic blessings in your lives. This ritual not only fosters appreciation for each other but also aligns your energies with the abundant flow of the universe.

Chakra Alignment Meditation for Couples:

Incorporate chakra alignment meditations into your routine. Sit comfortably together, focus on each chakra, and visualize a harmonious flow of energy between you. This practice promotes balance, understanding, and a shared sense of spiritual well-being.

These practices serve as cosmic bridges, connecting partners in a shared exploration of the divine dance of existence. As you integrate these rituals into your relationship, may the cosmic energy envelop you both, guiding your journey toward profound connection, growth, and everlasting love.

## Cosmic Energy in the Home

Cosmic energy subtly shapes the energetic ambiance of our homes, influencing not just our personal practices but the overall atmosphere of living spaces. It's a dance of vibrancy, balance, and interconnectedness that unfolds in every corner.

Consider the arrangement and decor of your living spaces as an invitation to cosmic energy. Integrate natural materials, plants, and symbols that align with principles of balance and harmony. This thoughtful curation establishes an environment in resonance with cosmic forces.

Harness the power of crystals and sacred objects to infuse your home with cosmic energy. Strategically placing crystals enhances specific energies, while symbols or objects with cosmic significance contribute to the overall energetic resonance.

Regularly cleanse the energy of your home through cosmic rituals. Utilize smudging with sage or palo santo, employ saltwater for purification, or introduce sound vibrations like singing bowls to dispel stagnant energy and welcome fresh cosmic currents.

Consider the influence of lighting on your home's energetic ambiance. Embrace natural light and incorporate soft, warm-toned lighting during the evening, aligning your living spaces with the natural rhythms of the universe.

Adorn your walls with cosmic art and symbols that echo your spiritual journey. Mandalas, sacred geometry, or celestial motifs serve as visual anchors, elevating the energy of your home and infusing it with cosmic inspiration.

Create dedicated sacred spaces or altars within your home that resonate with cosmic energy. Choose a focal point for items holding personal or spiritual significance and engage with this space through practices like meditation, intention setting, or moments of reflection.

Integrate cosmic soundscapes into your home environment. Play soft, meditative music or ambient sounds inspired by nature, enhancing the energetic flow and vibrational quality of your living spaces.

By consciously infusing your home with cosmic energy, you transform it into a haven of balance, inspiration, and spiritual nourishment. Every chosen element, ritual, and intention contributes to the cosmic symphony, inviting a harmonious dance of energies aligned with the vast rhythms of the universe.

Establishing a living space in harmonious resonance with cosmic energy involves a mindful and intentional approach. Below are some insightful tips to cultivate an environment that seamlessly integrates the cosmic dance of energy into your home:

1. Clutter Clearance:

Commence the process by decluttering your living spaces. The presence of clutter can impede the free flow of energy, creating stagnant areas. Keep your surroundings organized and free from unnecessary items to allow energy to move freely.

1. Natural Elements:

Embrace the natural elements within your home. Integrate plants, natural materials, and stones that hold cosmic significance. These elements not only enhance the aesthetic beauty of your space but also connect it to the grounding energies of the Earth.

1. Sacred Symbols:

Infuse your home with sacred symbols and cosmic motifs. Mandalas, yantras, or symbols from various spiritual traditions can serve as powerful anchors for cosmic energy. Place them strategically in areas where you spend time or engage in spiritual practices.

1. Balance of Energies:

Aim for a balanced energy flow in each room. Consider the principles of feng shui or other energy-balancing philosophies to arrange furniture and decor in a way that promotes harmonious energy circulation. Pay attention to the placement of mirrors, as they can reflect and enhance energy.

1. Cleansing Rituals:

Regularly perform cleansing rituals to purify the energy in your home. Smudging with sage or palo santo, using saltwater sprays, or employing sound vibrations with instruments like singing bowls can clear stagnant energy and invite fresh cosmic currents.

1. Intentional Lighting:

Be mindful of the lighting in your home. Natural light is ideal, so maximize the use of windows during the day. In the evening, opt for warm-toned lighting to create a cozy and calming atmosphere aligned with the cosmic rhythms.

1. Personalized Altars:

Create personalized altars or sacred spaces within your home. Dedicate these spaces to your spiritual practices, incorporating items of personal or cosmic significance. Engage with these altars through meditation, prayer, or moments of quiet reflection.

1. Cosmic Artistry:

Choose artwork that resonates with cosmic themes. Whether it's paintings, sculptures, or other forms of art, select pieces that inspire a sense of wonder and connection to the cosmos. These visuals can uplift the energy of your living spaces.

1. Mindful Soundscapes:

Integrate mindful soundscapes into your home environment. Play soft, meditative music, or incorporate sounds of nature to enhance the vibrational quality of your living spaces. These sounds can attune your space to cosmic frequencies.

1. Energetic Boundaries:

Establish energetic boundaries within your home. Consider using crystals or plants to create energetic barriers in areas where privacy and protection are desired. These boundaries can define and enhance specific energetic qualities.

By incorporating these tips into your home, you create a living space that not only reflects your personal style but also resonates with the cosmic energies that weave through the universe.

Each intentional choice contributes to the vibrancy and harmony of your home, fostering an environment conducive to spiritual growth and well-being.

In our quest to integrate cosmic energy into our daily lives, advanced concepts emerge to elevate the vibrational resonance of our living spaces. Crystals, with their unique vibrational frequencies, serve as potent conduits for cosmic energy. Thoughtfully placing these gems aligns their energies with specific intentions, creating an environment resonant with cosmic currents. Regular rituals for cleansing and programming ensure that crystals consistently radiate cosmic energy, enriched with our chosen qualities.

Space clearing rituals play a crucial role in maintaining energetic equilibrium within our living environments. Practices such as singing bowl ceremonies, salt rituals, or intentional settings contribute to clearing residual energies and invite the revitalizing flow of cosmic currents. By engaging in these rituals regularly, we not only foster vibrancy but also keep our homes attuned to the cosmic dance.

Feng Shui, an ancient Chinese practice, provides an additional layer to harmonizing our living spaces with cosmic energy. It involves the intentional arrangement of furniture, colors, and elements to optimize the flow of energy, or "Qi." By aligning our homes with the principles of Feng Shui, we enhance the cosmic resonance within our living spaces, promoting balance, prosperity, and well-being.

These practices offer tangible and transformative experiences within the spaces we inhabit daily, fostering a deeper resonance with the cosmic forces that guide our journey of

self-discovery and connection. As we embark on the exploration of these advanced concepts, we unveil more profound insights into the cosmic tapestry. The forthcoming chapters promise a deeper dive into advanced cosmic energy practices, unveiling the mysteries that lie at the intersection of cosmic forces and our individual existence.

# 8

## ADVANCED CONCEPTS IN COSMIC ENERGY

Embarking on the exploration of advanced concepts in cosmic energy invites us to transcend the boundaries of conventional understanding, delving into realms that unveil the intricate connections between the cosmos and our individual lives.

Astrology, an ancient and intricate system, is the study of celestial bodies' positions and their influence on human affairs. It operates on the belief that the positions of planets and stars at the time of one's birth can offer insights into personality, relationships, and life events. By decoding the language of the stars, Astrology becomes a tool for self-discovery, helping individuals navigate the cosmic energies shaping their destinies.

The rhythmic pulse of Cosmic Cycles echoes through the vast expanse of the universe, influencing the ebb and flow of energy. These cycles, often linked to celestial events, seasons, or planetary alignments, carry unique vibrational frequencies that impact personal and collective consciousness. Understanding and attuning to these cycles can empower individuals to harness the prevailing cosmic energies for personal growth, manifestation, and spiritual evolution.

The Akashic Records, often described as an ethereal library of universal knowledge, store the collective wisdom of every soul's journey throughout time. Accessing the Akashic Records involves tapping into the energetic imprints of past, present, and future possibilities. This profound exploration allows individuals to gain insights into their life purpose, unresolved karmic patterns, and the broader tapestry of their soul's evolution.

The concept of Past Lives suggests that our souls undergo a series of reincarnations, each lifetime contributing to our spiritual growth and understanding. Exploring past lives involves delving into the memories and experiences that transcend our current existence. This exploration can provide valuable insights into recurring patterns, relationships, and unresolved lessons, offering a deeper understanding of one's spiritual journey.

As we navigate these advanced cosmic concepts, the chapters that follow will unravel the intricacies of each, guiding us toward a more profound connection with the cosmic forces shaping our existence. May this journey be one of enlightenment, self-discovery, and a harmonious alignment with the cosmic dance of energy that surrounds us.

## Astrology and Cosmic Cycles

Astrology, an ancient and enduring system, traces its roots to the observations of celestial movements by early civilizations, including the Babylonians, Egyptians, and Mesopotamians. These cultures carefully recorded the rhythmic dance of planets and stars, linking these cosmic events to earthly occurrences and human destinies.

At its essence, astrology proposes a profound connection between the vast cosmos and individual lives on Earth. This concept posits that the positions of celestial bodies at the time of one's birth can offer profound insights into their personality, characteristics, and life trajectory.

The zodiac, a twelve-part division of the night sky, serves as astrology's foundational framework. Each segment corresponds to specific constellations, forming astrological signs that signify distinct personality traits. Further, these signs are organized into houses, governing particular life aspects like relationships, career, and spirituality.

The planets, acting as cosmic messengers, traverse the zodiac, influencing the energies of the signs and houses they inhabit. Each planet carries unique qualities and vibrations, contributing to the cosmic symphony shaping individual experiences. The arrangement of planets during birth creates a natal or birth chart, an individualized map revealing the imprints of cosmic energies on their journey.

Astrology serves as a powerful tool for self-discovery, enabling individuals to comprehend their strengths, challenges, and life purpose. By exploring the cosmic energies embedded in their birth chart, individuals gain awareness to navigate life's challenges and align themselves with the universal forces guiding their path. The upcoming chapters will delve deeper into the intricate language of astrology, unraveling its complexities and revealing the cosmic wisdom it holds.

Engaging with the intricate dance of planetary movements and moon cycles within the realm of astrology provides a profound opportunity to align with cosmic energy and navigate life's ebb and flow. The dynamic interplay of planets and the rhythmic dance of the moon create energetic currents that significantly influence our experiences on Earth.

Planetary movements, known as transits, continually shape the cosmic energy available to us. As planets traverse through different zodiac signs and houses, they form aspects with each other, generating unique energy signatures. Understanding these transits empowers individuals to navigate prevailing energies, offering valuable insights for informed decision-making.

Retrogrades, where a planet appears to move backward in its orbit, represent periods of reflection and reassessment. These phases prompt us to delve into internal realms, revisiting aspects of our lives to facilitate personal growth and transformation.

Moon cycles, a fundamental aspect of astrology, hold distinct energies throughout their phases.

The New Moon marks the beginning of the lunar cycle, inviting introspection and

intention-setting. As the moon waxes, it carries the energy of new beginnings. Conversely, the Full Moon signifies culmination and fruition, illuminating areas of our lives with clarity and insight. Lunar eclipses, powerful celestial events intensifying the energy of Full Moons, often coincide with significant life shifts, encouraging us to embrace transformation and align with our authentic path.

Working with planetary movements and moon cycles requires mindful observation and intentional practices. By attuning ourselves to the cosmic energies revealed through astrology, we gain a deeper understanding of the universal forces shaping our journey. This conscious alignment allows us to flow with the currents of cosmic energy, fostering personal growth and navigating life's cycles with grace.

## Akashic Records and Past Lives

The concept of Akashic Records and Past Lives in New Age philosophy offers a profound exploration into the metaphysical dimensions of individual and collective existence. Rooted in ancient spiritual traditions and gaining prominence within the New Age movement, these ideas provide a unique perspective through which seekers can delve into the mysteries of cosmic energy.

Akashic Records, originating from Sanskrit terminology, refer to an ethereal repository of knowledge imprinted on the fabric of the universe. This universal database is often envisioned as a non-physical library containing the experiences, thoughts, and emotions of every soul throughout time. The term "Akasha" symbolizes the primordial cosmic energy, and accessing the Akashic Records is believed to unveil the past, present, and potential future of a soul's journey.

In New Age philosophy, the Akashic Records serve as a cosmic compendium, documenting the soul's evolution across various lifetimes. Practitioners often perceive these records as a source of profound guidance, offering insights into life purposes, karmic patterns, and opportunities for growth. Accessing the Akashic Records is thought to be achievable through deep meditation, psychic intuition, or with the assistance of trained practitioners skilled in Akashic readings.

Past Lives, intimately connected with the Akashic Records, propose that our souls have traversed multiple lifetimes, each contributing to our present incarnation. This cyclical journey of birth, death, and rebirth is central to the concept of reincarnation, embraced by various spiritual traditions worldwide.

In New Age thought, past life regression is a technique that allows individuals to explore their previous incarnations. Through guided meditation or hypnosis, seekers tap into the memories stored in their subconscious, unraveling the threads of past experiences that may influence their current life. The understanding is that by gaining insights into past lives, individuals can heal unresolved issues, overcome recurring challenges, and accelerate their spiritual evolution.

The exploration of Akashic Records and past lives within New Age philosophy provides a holistic framework for understanding the interconnected nature of cosmic energy. By delving into the timeless realms of the Akashic Records and acknowledging the continuity of the soul's journey through past lives, seekers aim to harmonize with the cosmic currents, ultimately fostering

self-discovery and spiritual enlightenment.

The exploration of Akashic Records and past lives for personal growth is a transformative venture rooted in deep introspection and spiritual practices. Individuals embark on this journey for diverse reasons, ranging from understanding current challenges to unveiling latent talents and potentials.

Meditation and Mindfulness: A primary gateway to accessing the Akashic Records and exploring past lives involves meditation and mindfulness practices. By calming the mind, individuals create a receptive space for intuitive insights. Regular meditation, especially focusing on connecting with the higher self, can facilitate a profound understanding of the soul's journey.

Past Life Regression Therapy: Trained past life regression therapists offer a structured approach to exploring past lives. Through techniques like hypnosis, individuals can access memories and experiences from previous incarnations. This therapeutic method allows for the healing of unresolved issues, traumas, and the integration of lessons learned across lifetimes.

Intuitive Practices: Developing and trusting intuitive abilities is another avenue for delving into the Akashic Records. Working with divination tools, such as pendulums or tarot cards, helps individuals tap into their innate psychic abilities. This intuitive exploration offers glimpses into past lives and provides guidance for present challenges.

Dreamwork: Dreams are considered windows to the subconscious, potentially holding clues to past life experiences. Maintaining a dream journal and paying attention to recurring themes or symbols can offer insights into the soul's journey. Techniques like lucid dreaming may be employed to consciously explore past life memories during dream states.

Energy Healing and Reiki: Engaging in energy healing practices, like Reiki, facilitates a deeper connection with the universal life force. Practitioners often report accessing insights into their soul's journey and receiving guidance from higher realms during energy healing sessions. The heightened vibrational state induced by these practices can open doors to profound spiritual experiences.

Akashic Record Readings: Seeking the assistance of a skilled intuitive or Akashic Records reader directly explores one's records. These practitioners can access the Akashic field and provide insights into past lives, karmic patterns, and life purposes. The guidance received in these readings serves as a valuable tool for personal growth.

The journey of exploring Akashic Records and past lives is deeply personal, requiring patience, self-reflection, and spiritual dedication. As individuals connect with the timeless dimensions of their existence, they find valuable lessons, healing opportunities, and a greater sense of purpose unfolding in their current lives.

As we bring our exploration of advanced cosmic energy concepts to a close, we stand on the brink of spiritual discovery, where the intricacies of astrology, cosmic cycles, Akashic Records, and past lives have unveiled profound aspects of our cosmic journey. Each of these advanced concepts acts as a guide, providing insights into the mysteries of our existence and the cosmic forces that influence our paths.

The celestial dance of the stars, the exploration of past lives, and the wisdom held within the Akashic Records offer a rich tapestry of knowledge and transformative potential. These realms beckon us to dive deeper into the essence of our souls, encouraging self-discovery and a connection with the cosmic energies that shape our destinies.

As we transition to the forthcoming chapter, "Continuing the Spiritual Journey," we carry the acquired wisdom forward, ready to embrace further self-discovery and spiritual growth. The upcoming journey promises revelations, heightened awareness, and a harmonious dance with the cosmic forces that weave through the universe.

Prepare to step into the next phase of your spiritual quest, where the threads of existence lead to profound insights and a deepened connection with the energies permeating the universe.

The forthcoming chapter will serve as guides, offering practices and wisdom to navigate your spiritual journey with purpose and clarity. May the cosmic energy's wisdom be your steadfast companion as you explore the unfolding chapters of your spiritual path.

# 9

## CONTINUING YOUR SPIRITUAL JOURNEY

As we embark on Chapter 8, "Continuing Your Spiritual Journey," we are poised to explore the multifaceted resources that enrich the ongoing quest for self-discovery. In this segment of the journey, we delve into the importance of personal growth, drawing insights from various sources that illuminate the path ahead. The decision to continue our spiritual odyssey is not merely a choice; it is an intentional commitment to becoming a beacon of cosmic energy, radiating wisdom, harmony, and connection.

One invaluable resource on this journey is the wealth of spiritual literature that spans diverse traditions and philosophies. These texts act as guides, offering profound insights, timeless wisdom, and the collective experiences of seekers who have navigated similar paths. Engaging with these writings becomes a sacred dialogue, enriching our understanding and providing nourishment for the soul.

Equally crucial to our ongoing exploration is the significance of personal growth. Beyond the acquisition of knowledge, true spiritual evolution involves a continuous process of self-reflection, self-awareness, and intentional transformation. Through practices such as meditation, mindfulness, and self-inquiry, we navigate the inner landscapes of our being, fostering a harmonious alignment with the cosmic energies that permeate the universe.

Becoming a beacon of cosmic energy involves not only personal growth but also a commitment to sharing the light of wisdom with others. As we advance on our spiritual journey, we recognize the interconnectedness of all beings and understand that our individual growth contributes to the collective elevation of consciousness. By embodying the principles of compassion, empathy, and service, we become conduits for the expansive and transformative energies that flow through the cosmos.

In the chapters that follow, we will explore practices, reflections, and insights that guide us in embracing the ever-unfolding dimensions of our spiritual journey. Together, let us illuminate the path with the radiant energy of wisdom, inviting others to join us in the pursuit of a harmonious and interconnected existence.

## Further Learning and Exploration

Embarking on an enriched journey of continuous learning and exploration in the realm of New Age practices and cosmic energy calls for a treasury of insightful resources. Here are some valuable recommendations to illuminate your path:

1. "The Power of Now" by Eckhart Tolle:

    - Why it's invaluable: Eckhart Tolle's profound reflections on consciousness and the present moment are foundational for spiritual seekers. "The Power of Now" offers practical wisdom for living mindfully, harmonizing with the essence of cosmic energy.

2. "The Celestine Prophecy" by James Redfield:

- Why it's invaluable: This spiritual adventure novel introduces synchronicity and interconnectedness. "The Celestine Prophecy" acts as a guide to understanding spiritual dimensions and the flow of cosmic energy in our lives.

3. "Autobiography of a Yogi" by Paramahansa Yogananda:

- Why it's invaluable: Yogananda's autobiography delves into yogic practices, meditation, and the awakening of cosmic energy within. It provides profound insights into the mystical realms and the spiritual journey.

4. "The Secret" by Rhonda Byrne:

- Why it's invaluable: "The Secret" popularized the Law of Attraction, exploring how thoughts and energy shape our reality. This book equips readers with practical tools for manifesting positive change through alignment with cosmic energy.

5. "Wheels of Life" by Anodea Judith:

- Why it's invaluable: Anodea Judith's work on the chakra system is a comprehensive guide to understanding and balancing the energy centers. "Wheels of Life" facilitates the harmonious flow of cosmic energy throughout mind, body, and spirit.

6. "The Law of One" (Ra Material):

    ◦ Why it's invaluable: This channeled series offers metaphysical insights into the universe, cosmic energy, and consciousness evolution. It deepens understanding of interconnectedness and our role in the cosmic tapestry.

7. Online Courses and Workshops:

    ◦ Why they're invaluable: Platforms like Udemy, Coursera, and Insight Timer offer diverse online courses on meditation, energy healing, and New Age philosophies. These courses provide interactive learning experiences, aiding in the practical application of cosmic energy principles.

8. Local Spiritual Communities and Retreats:

    ◦ Why they're invaluable: Engaging with local spiritual communities, workshops, or retreats provides hands-on experiences and connections with like-minded individuals. These environments offer support, guidance, and a sense of community in your spiritual journey.

These resources span foundational teachings to practical applications, offering diverse perspectives to tailor your exploration. Trust your intuition in selecting resources that deeply resonate with you as you navigate the unique journey of continuous spiritual growth. May these insights become guiding lights on your path to self-discovery and cosmic connection.

Embarking on a continuous spiritual journey involves embracing the mindset of perpetual learning, a guiding beacon that illuminates the path toward a deeper connection with cosmic energies. The New Age community, a diverse tapestry of seekers, provides avenues for personal growth and connection, nurturing a shared exploration of the profound mysteries of existence.

One impactful avenue for growth is participation in spiritual workshops and retreats. These immersive experiences offer hands-on practices, guided meditations, and opportunities to connect with seasoned practitioners. Workshops and retreats serve as environments for deepening one's understanding of cosmic energy and fostering connections with fellow seekers on similar paths.

Engaging in online forums and discussion groups amplifies the collective wisdom within the New Age community. These platforms serve as spaces for sharing experiences, asking questions, and gaining insights from diverse perspectives. The exchange of ideas not only broadens understanding but also creates a sense of shared exploration among like-minded individuals.

Exploration of advanced practices within New Age spirituality is a natural progression for those seeking to delve deeper. Concepts such as astral projection, energy medicine, and sacred geometry offer new dimensions for exploration. Seeking out resources, books, and courses aligned with evolving interests broadens the scope of one's spiritual journey.

Building connections with like-minded souls is a vital aspect of sustained spiritual growth. Attending local meetups, spiritual gatherings, or virtual events facilitates the creation of a supportive network. These connections provide opportunities for sharing insights, experiences, and mutual encouragement.

Crafting a personalized spiritual practice adds depth and authenticity to the journey. Tailoring routines to individual needs by incorporating practices like breathwork, sound healing, or intuitive arts ensures resonance with personal aspirations and ongoing growth.

Nature serves as a powerful spiritual guide, offering profound lessons in cosmic energy. Regularly connecting with the natural world through walks, hikes, or contemplative moments deepens one's understanding of the interconnected dance of existence, grounding the spiritual journey in the present moment.

Remaining open to new perspectives within the diverse New Age community is essential for continued growth. The community's richness lies in its diversity of beliefs and practices, offering opportunities to explore and understand perspectives that may differ from one's own.

As the spiritual journey unfolds, staying receptive to the flow of cosmic energy guides seekers toward new horizons of understanding and connection. Learning, sharing, and weaving a unique thread into the cosmic tapestry, the ongoing journey is a testament to the boundless wonders of the universe. May the path be adorned with wisdom, growth, and the continuous exploration of the profound mysteries that cosmic energy unfolds.

## Personal Growth and Transformation

Embarking on a spiritual journey invites individuals into a realm of profound personal growth and ongoing transformation. Within the embrace of cosmic energy, this transformative odyssey becomes a continuous exploration, a perpetual evolution of self-discovery. In navigating this journey, we delve into the essence of personal growth guided by the warmth and wisdom inherent in the transformative powers of cosmic energy.

At its core, personal growth within the context of cosmic energy involves a deep exploration of one's inner landscapes. Practices such as meditation, introspection, and mindfulness serve as pathways for seekers to venture into the depths of their thoughts, emotions, and beliefs. The light of consciousness illuminates these inner realms, providing clarity and insight that lays the foundation for transformative change.

Aligned with cosmic energy, personal growth necessitates a profound reevaluation of beliefs and patterns. Seekers are encouraged to question societal conditioning, fostering autonomy in shaping personal values. Liberation from mental and emotional constraints becomes integral to this transformative journey, signaling a departure from limiting beliefs towards expansive self-realization.

The transformative power of cosmic energy extends to emotional well-being. Energy healing and breathwork, practices that attune individuals to cosmic vibrations, become tools for releasing stagnant emotions and cultivating emotional resilience. As emotional blockages dissolve, an inner harmony emerges, contributing to personal growth and overall well-being.

In the pursuit of cosmic alignment, the physical body undergoes its own transformation. Practices such as yoga, tai chi, and conscious movement serve as gateways to attune the body to the flow of cosmic energy. This physical alignment enhances vitality and well-being, becoming a tangible expression of the transformative journey within.

In the exploration of cosmic energy, relationships also undergo a metamorphosis. Emphasizing interconnectedness, cosmic philosophy fosters compassion, empathy, and a deep appreciation for the sacredness of all life. This shift in perspective contributes to harmonious relationships and a sense of interconnectedness with the cosmic tapestry.

The journey of personal growth within cosmic energy is an ongoing process, a continuous spiral of evolution. Each experience, whether perceived as a challenge or a blessing, becomes a stepping stone toward greater self-realization. The transformative journey is marked by a willingness to embrace change, a commitment to self-discovery, and an openness to the infinite possibilities woven into the fabric of cosmic existence.

In essence, the cosmic journey is a sacred dance of growth and transformation, an exploration of the boundless potential residing within each individual. As seekers navigate the ebb and flow of cosmic energies, they actively participate in their own evolution, shaping a reality that aligns with the highest aspects of their being. May this transformative journey be a source of inspiration, resilience, and the continuous unfolding of the soul's potential.

Within the intricate tapestry of cosmic energy, the stories of individuals who have embraced transformative journeys stand as compelling testaments to the profound impact of aligning with cosmic energies.

One such narrative unfolds with Emma, an artist facing the stifling grip of self-doubt and creative stagnation. Engaging in practices like meditation and energy healing, Emma discovered a profound connection with cosmic energy. This newfound alignment became a catalyst, unlocking a wellspring of creativity within her. The once-muted colors on her canvas burst forth vibrantly, reflecting the confidence and self-expression bestowed upon her by cosmic alignment.

Another tale features John, a corporate professional entangled in the relentless demands of a fast-paced life. In the stillness of mindfulness, John uncovered the transformative potential of cosmic energy. Through dedicated practices like meditation and conscious breathing, he not only found relief from stress but also gained a deeper understanding of his purpose. Guided by cosmic energies, he made intentional choices, aligning his career with his passions and fostering a profound sense of fulfillment.

The journey of Sarah, a seeker of inner peace, provides insight into the transformative power of cosmic energy in emotional healing. Engaging in practices such as energy clearing and embracing the present moment, Sarah untangled the knots of past traumas. The cosmic currents of healing energy facilitated the mending of emotional wounds, paving the way for a renewed sense of joy and inner tranquility.

These narratives, intricately woven into the cosmic tapestry, showcase the diverse ways in which individuals have harnessed cosmic energy for personal growth and transformation. From unleashing creativity to navigating life's challenges with resilience, the common thread lies in the profound shifts that occur when one consciously aligns with the cosmic dance of existence.

As these stories unfold, they extend an invitation to others to embark on their transformative odysseys. The cosmic journey becomes a shared exploration, with each seeker contributing their unique notes to the symphony of cosmic energies. These tales illuminate the infinite possibilities inherent in aligning with the cosmic flow, reminding us that within the dance of cosmic energy, the potential for profound change is boundless. May these narratives inspire, guide, and ignite the flame of transformation within the hearts of those on their cosmic journey.

## Becoming a Beacon of Cosmic Energy

Starting on the path to become a beacon of cosmic energy invites a profound transformation that extends into every aspect of life. It is an endeavor to live in resonance with the universal energies that shape the fabric of existence. Imagine yourself as a radiant force, consciously attuning your thoughts, actions, and intentions to the harmonious frequencies of the cosmic dance.

In the realm of thoughts, strive to align your mental landscape with the interconnectedness of all things. Let your contemplations be infused with the awareness that each thought contributes to the collective consciousness. As you navigate the complexities of your mind, cultivate positivity, understanding, and a sense of interconnected wonder.

Translating cosmic insights into actions involves becoming a living embodiment of the boundless love and compassion present in the cosmic currents. Embrace the sacredness inherent in every moment, recognizing the dance of existence even in the simplest gestures. Extend kindness and empathy to others, becoming a conduit for the expansive energy that transcends individual boundaries.

Balance and harmony should be guiding principles in your decision-making process. In the grand tapestry of life, your choices contribute to the equilibrium or dissonance of the overall composition. Strive for decisions that reflect a conscious effort to create balance not only in your life but also in the lives of those you influence.

In the realm of relationships, aspire to become a source of inspiration. Encourage others to recognize the cosmic dance within themselves and celebrate the unique threads they bring to the collective tapestry. Create an environment where diversity is not only accepted but embraced, fostering unity in the shared experience of cosmic existence.

Becoming a beacon of cosmic energy isn't about monumental gestures; it's about embodying the subtle rhythms of daily living. Practice mindfulness in the gentle currents of your everyday

experiences, express gratitude through intentional breaths, and infuse positive intentions into the harmonious melodies of your actions.

As you navigate your existence, let the awareness of cosmic energy guide your interactions and decisions. Be a beacon that lights up the paths of others, showcasing the transformative journey that unfolds when one aligns with the cosmic dance. May your life be a testament to the profound impact of living in harmony with the cosmic energies that intricately weave through the tapestry of existence.

Embodying and sharing cosmic energy for the greater good is a deliberate commitment to contribute positively to the collective human experience. This involves a profound journey of self-awareness, where you explore the depths of your being, understanding both your strengths and weaknesses. Through self-reflection, you gain insight into your unique cosmic signature, aligning your actions with a broader cosmic purpose.

Authenticity is a central theme in this endeavor. Embracing your true self, acknowledging both light and shadow aspects, creates an authentic resonance that inspires others to do the same. In the cosmic dance, authenticity becomes a powerful force, harmonizing the collective by encouraging individuals to contribute their genuine essence.

Sharing cosmic energy necessitates extending principles of interconnectedness and compassion to the world. Acts of kindness, whether through helping hands or comforting words, become channels for cosmic energy, creating positive ripples that touch others. Global consciousness amplifies impact, recognizing the interconnectedness of humanity and actively supporting initiatives for unity, peace, and environmental sustainability.

Education and inspiration are vital aspects of sharing cosmic energy. Offering guidance and sharing experiences encourage others to embark on their transformative journeys. Through mentorship or leading by example, you become a beacon illuminating the path for others, fostering a collective awakening to cosmic forces.

Collaboration with like-minded individuals enhances the impact of efforts. Joining forces with those who share a vision creates a collective influence, contributing to the co-creation of a reality infused with cosmic harmony. Collective action becomes a potent vehicle for manifesting positive change globally.

In the grand symphony of existence, embodying and sharing cosmic energy is an ongoing commitment, extending far beyond personal boundaries. Radiating the transformative power of cosmic insights into the world contributes to the flourishing of humanity and the planet. May this journey be filled with purpose, love, and the radiant energy of cosmic harmony.

# 10

## Conclusion

As we stand at the conclusion of "Harnessing Cosmic Energy: A Beginner's Guide to New Age Spiritual Practices," let's reflect on the profound odyssey we've undertaken together.

Throughout this transformative journey, we navigated the intricate landscape of New Age spirituality, witnessing the harmonious convergence of ancient wisdom and contemporary practices.

Our exploration commenced with a deep dive into the roots of New Age spirituality, tracing its emergence from a wave of spiritual curiosity in the mid-20th century. The movement's evolution unfolded before us, shaped by a melding of Eastern philosophies, Western mysticism, and indigenous traditions, resulting in a vibrant tapestry of diverse beliefs and practices.

Venturing into the core principles of New Age philosophy, we unraveled a holistic worldview that celebrated personal transformation, interconnectedness, and the cosmic dance of life. This exploration unveiled the myriad influences, from Eastern philosophies to indigenous traditions, contributing to the movement's distinctive spiritual perspective.

The heart of our journey led us into the intricate realm of cosmic energy, the universal life force binding all living things. Practices such as meditation, energy healing, and attunement emerged as gateways to enhancing our connection with this cosmic force, fostering personal transformation and a profound understanding of our existence.

Our quest deepened as we explored the multifaceted nature of cosmic energy, recognizing its influence not only in the physical realm but also in the realms of emotion, thought, and spirit. Consciously aligning with universal currents became the key to unlocking boundless possibilities within the intricate tapestry of existence.

Chapters unfolded seamlessly, delving into meditation, visualization, and the understanding of chakras, offering practical guidance for beginners to attune themselves to cosmic energy.

Integration into daily life became a central theme, fostering harmony in relationships and infusing cosmic energy into the sanctuary of our homes.

Venturing into advanced concepts, we glimpsed the interconnected dance of celestial bodies, delved into the Akashic Records, and explored the profound impact of past lives on our present journey. These advanced concepts served as doorways to deeper self-exploration and growth, expanding our understanding of the cosmic tapestry.

As we approach the conclusion of this enlightening journey, let's carry forward the wisdom gleaned from these pages. May the resonance of cosmic energy guide us in ongoing spiritual exploration, encouraging personal growth, interconnectedness, and a harmonious existence.

# HARNESSING COSMIC ENERGY

This guide is a stepping stone in your spiritual journey. Whether you are a seeker taking your first steps or an experienced traveler on this path, the invitation is extended: continue to explore, learn, and embody the radiant energy of the cosmos. May your journey be filled with discovery, transformation, and a profound connection to the cosmic symphony that dances through the tapestry of existence.

As we stand at the culmination of our exploration into the realms of cosmic energy, we find ourselves surrounded by the echoes of wisdom and the gentle whispers of a universal force that transcends time and space. Throughout this transformative journey, we have delved into the heart of New Age spirituality, unveiling the intricate tapestry woven with threads of interconnectedness, personal transformation, and the radiant dance of cosmic energy.

The journey began by unraveling the key principles of New Age philosophy—a celebration of global spiritual wisdom, an exploration of diverse cultures, and an invitation to find one's unique path within the interconnected tapestry of human spirituality. From the fusion of Eastern philosophies and indigenous traditions to the echoes of counterculture movements, we discovered the diverse influences shaping New Age thought and fostering ideals of personal freedom, self-expression, and holistic well-being.

Our exploration deepened as we immersed ourselves in the profound concept of cosmic energy—a universal life force that permeates every facet of existence, connecting all living things to the cosmic dance. Attuning ourselves to this dynamic force through practices like meditation, energy healing, and the recognition of its subtle influence on our emotions and thoughts, we embarked on a transformative journey towards higher states of consciousness and interconnected wonder.

As we ventured into the nature of cosmic energy within the New Age perspective, we discovered its role as a guiding light shaping the landscape of spirituality. This intricate dance of existence, where the threads of our being are woven into the cosmic tapestry, became a profound invitation to explore the boundless possibilities within the interconnected web of life.

Delving into practical aspects, we explored meditation as a gateway to cosmic energy, unlocking its potential to foster harmony and elevate consciousness. Techniques such as visualization practices and engagement with the chakra system provided practical pathways to attune ourselves to the cosmic currents and enhance our overall well-being.

Our journey extended to the realm of cosmic energy healing practices, where we witnessed the transformative potential of modalities like Reiki, Qi Gong, and Pranic Healing. The understanding of self-healing techniques and practices for maintaining energetic health illuminated the path towards holistic well-being.

In the chapter on Manifesting with Cosmic Energy, we navigated the intricate relationship between cosmic energy, the Law of Attraction, and the creation of abundance. Exploring

practical steps for manifestation and cultivating an abundance mindset, we discovered the intimate connection between our intentions, thoughts, and the cosmic forces at play.

The exploration of advanced concepts opened doors to Astrology, Cosmic Cycles, Akashic Records, and Past Lives. Originating from ancient wisdom, these concepts offered deeper insights into the cosmic dance, planetary movements, and the profound exploration of personal histories through the Akashic Records.

As we conclude this journey, the importance of integrating these practices into daily life becomes evident. Creating harmonious routines, fostering connectivity in relationships, and embracing cosmic energy within the home provide a tangible foundation for the ongoing spiritual journey.

The final chapters encourage us to continue the exploration, offering resources for deeper study, insights into personal growth, and the embodiment of cosmic energy in our daily lives. Becoming a beacon of cosmic energy emerges as an inspiring call, inviting us to live in alignment with our understanding of the interconnected web that unites us all.

In this concluding chapter, we've touched upon the vast landscapes of cosmic energy—a force that not only shapes our personal journey but resonates on a global scale, contributing to the collective evolution of consciousness. As you step forward, may the wisdom gathered from these pages accompany you, guiding you towards a life filled with purpose, connection, and the radiant energy of the cosmic symphony.

As we stand at the crossroads of this transformative journey, let the wisdom unveiled throughout this exploration resonate in the very fabric of your being. The cosmic energy, which has been our guiding light, now beckons you to translate this knowledge into conscious and intentional living.

Reflect on the profound revelations that cosmic energy is not an abstract concept but a dynamic force intricately woven into the tapestry of existence. As you conclude this exploration, consider the following call to action, allowing the pulsating rhythms of the cosmos to infuse every facet of your life:

Conscious Living: Approach each moment with a heightened awareness, recognizing the subtle dance of cosmic energy in the mundane and the extraordinary. Let conscious living be the cornerstone of your journey.

Meditative Practices: Cultivate a regular meditation practice as a sacred space for cosmic energy to flow harmoniously. In the stillness, unveil the depths of your being and attune yourself to the cosmic currents.

Energy Alignment: Explore various practices that align your energy with the universal forces. Whether through meditation, visualization, or energy healing, find modalities that resonate with your essence, allowing cosmic energy to flow unimpeded.

Manifest with Intention: Apply the principles of manifestation with positivity and intention. Understand the powerful influence of your thoughts and intentions, directing them consciously to shape a reality filled with abundance, joy, and purpose.

Connect with Nature: Recognize nature as a profound expression of cosmic energy. Spend time outdoors, connect with the elements, and witness the intricate dance of life. Align yourself with the larger cosmic symphony.

Radiate Compassion: Extend the interconnectedness you've discovered within your interactions with others. Radiate compassion, kindness, and understanding, recognizing the shared cosmic essence that unites us all.

Create Harmonious Spaces: Infuse your living spaces with the harmonious energy of cosmic forces. Through the thoughtful use of crystals, space clearing, or Feng Shui, create environments resonating with the vibrancy of the cosmic dance.

Continue the Journey: The closing of this chapter marks the beginning of a lifelong journey. Keep exploring, learning, and evolving. Dive deeper into the mysteries of cosmic energy, spirituality, and self-discovery.

Go forth on this adventure with an open heart and a mindful spirit. You're not just a traveler in this cosmic symphony but an integral note, contributing a unique melody to the grand composition of existence. May your journey be filled with the radiant energy of cosmic wisdom, guiding you toward a life resonating with harmony, purpose, and boundless connection.

www.ingramcontent.com/pod-product-compliance
Lightning Source LLC
LaVergne TN
LVHW020444070526
838199LV00063B/4846